THE EXPANDING CIRCLE

MATIAS OBLUDZYNER

The
EXPANDING
CIRCLE

HOW GENUINE LEADERS CONNECT WITH
THEMSELVES, CONNECT WITH OTHERS, AND
MAKE A DIFFERENCE.

First paperback edition: September 2020
ISBN: 979-8-6815-0175-6

Editor - Jillian West
Book designer - Jeanine Delay
Research and project manager - Michelle Mancher

www.matioblu.com

To Michelle, my amazing wife, and Eli, our wonderful son.

ACKNOWLEDGMENTS

This book wouldn't have been possible without the enduring support of my wife, Michelle. She served as an exemplary project manager while lending her prodigious research and writing skills to the crafting of the book. She brainstormed with me, provided thoughtful advice, and encouraged me throughout the process. I am fortunate to be married to such an amazing and loving woman.

I am immensely in debt to Jillian West, my editor. She has been much more than an outstanding editor; she has been a thoughtful, perceptive, and committed partner. She dug deep into the subject matter, offered guidance, and challenged me to develop the best possible product. Much of the good in the book is her doing. It was a total pleasure sharing this project with her.

I am deeply grateful to Jeanine Delay, the book's graphic designer, my former colleague at the World Bank Group, and my friend. She is capable of grasping the most complex issues and creating visual designs to make them easy to understand—all done with style and sophistication.

I also want to thank my friend, Paul McClure. He helped me think through the book and provided feedback to numerous drafts. More importantly, he has been my writing coach for many years. He taught me that writing in English—or in any language—is, above all, a thinking exercise.

I am grateful to Tom Haran, my friend and mentor. He has been a wonderful source of wisdom about leadership and relationship building, and reviewed several drafts of the book. I also want to thank Nicolas Dei Castelli and Max Mancher, both of whom provided thoughtful feedback and advice on the manuscript. I have been fortunate to have had amazing, generous mentors over the years. I discussed the book with many of them and learned much of what I know about leadership and communications from them. I want to especially thank Oscar Chemerinski, Alzbeta Klein, Lucie Blyth, and Sita Ramaswami. I also want to thank some amazing friends and colleagues—many of them outstanding leaders themselves—for their continuous support: Bill Adams, Matias Averbuj, Hernan Dobry, Claudio Epelman, Fabian Koss, Patricia Macchi, Veronica Machtey, Damian Raber, Cesar Rosenstein, Cristian Santillan, Michael Shifter, Nelson Waisberg, and Victoria Wigodzky.

I want to thank my brothers, Alejandro and Mariano. And I am deeply grateful to Michelle's family, whose support has been critical for us to spend time in Argentina where I wrote this book. Thanks to Kenny Mancher, Julie Mancher, Zach Mancher, Rachel Sier, Ruth Najjar, and Elisha Najjar.

I have interviewed more than three dozen leaders and talented professionals for this book. Their input has been critical and some of their stories became the case studies featured in the book. I am grateful to all of them for their time and generosity in helping me make this book a reality. In particular, I would like to thank David Auerbach, Rayco Bejarano, Diego Bekerman, Norma Gonzales, Sam Hendel, Fabrizio Hochschild, Avi Hoffman, Alzbeta Klein, Fabian Koss, Rachel Kyte, Carolina Larreira, and Frank Taverner.

Finally, I want to thank Renata De Verthelyi and Mariana Niemtzoff for their long-time support.

CONTENTS

INTRODUCTION 1

THE EXPANDING CIRCLE FRAMEWORK 9
The Need for Genuine Leadership 11
Communicating and Building Relationships 13

THE INNER CIRCLE 17
Defining Your Values, Ambitions and Goals 19
Learning from Mistakes—The Case of Diego 21
Developing Your Personal Narrative 26
A Window to Connect—The Case of Rachel 31

THE OUTER CIRCLE 37
Meaningful Connections 39
Building Relationships with the Right Mindset 43
Bridging Opportunities—The Case of Fabian 46
Fostering Trust—The Case of Avi and Frank 52
Developing a Shared Narrative 58
Be the Flow—The Case of Alzbeta 63
Connecting across Cultures 69
A One-Way Ticket—The Case of David 73
Building Your Network of Trusted Advisors 79
Beginning with Curiosity—The Case of Rayco 83
A Different Take on Networking—The Case of Sam 89

LOOKING BACK, LOOKING FORWARD 93

APPENDIX 103
Complex Ideas: Simple Presentations 105

ENDNOTES 111

REFERENCES 115

INTERVIEWS 121

ABOUT THE EDITOR 123

INTRODUCTION

A dream you dream alone is only a dream. A dream you dream together is reality.
—*John Lennon*

As we look ahead into the next century, leaders will be those who empower others.
—*Bill Gates*

The most dangerous leadership myth is that leaders are born— that there is a genetic factor to leadership. That's nonsense; in fact, the opposite is true. Leaders are made rather than born.
—*Warren Bennis*

I n 1999, the nation of East Timor became independent after more than two decades of Indonesian occupation. But independence came with a price. The country had suffered a total economic collapse, and civil war had left more than 200,000 dead. Another 300,000 had been forced to flee into West Timor. The United Nations had assumed full governing authority, and was in need of a leader to help the country chart a path towards democracy.

They chose Sérgio Vieira de Mello, a UN diplomat with more than three decades of experience in some of the most difficult places on the globe.

Described as part James Bond, part Bobby Kennedy, Sérgio was idealistic and pragmatic, and had an amazing capacity to connect with people. Originally from Brazil, Sérgio studied philosophy at the Sorbonne. There, he discovered anti-imperialist ideas, and was arrested for participating in the May 1968 demonstrations that rocked France. After completing his studies, Sérgio landed a position at the United Nations High Commissioner for Refugees, the UN agency responsible for protecting the rights of refugees. And over time, he built a reputation for expertly negotiating with donor governments, local political factions, and guerrilla groups. It was because of this reputation that he was chosen for the job in East Timor.

Sérgio's mission there was to foster security and stability, create political institutions and establish a civil administration, and set the basis for economic development—all from scratch. Inevitably, he and his team would make mistakes. But he knew that no matter how much formal authority the UN had given him, he had to work with the local leadership and community.

Xanana Gusmão, a former rebel commander and the unquestioned leader of the East Timorese people, was far from pleased with the UN involvement. He and his resistance movement hadn't risked their lives for years to have another group of foreigners take power. They were committed to a truly sovereign East Timor.

So when on his second day in Dili (East Timor's capital), after a 24-hour flight to get to the country, Sérgio made the additional two-hour journey to meet Xanana in his home, Xanana took notice. "I had expected to go down to Dili to see him, so I took note when Sérgio went out of his way to come see me."[1] This was the first of many encounters between the two men. Xanana told him about the East Timorese people and their long search for independence, and Sérgio shared his own story—as a native of Brazil (another developing nation), a young activist and demonstrator, and a UN professional working in war-torn areas.

"Sérgio and Xanana grew close; they liked to joke and tease each other," recalled Fabrizio Hochschild-Drummond, Sérgio's chief of staff in East Timor. "More important, Xanana felt respected by Sérgio. If they attended a ceremony, Sérgio—who held the formal authority—would give Xanana the spotlight."

But the burgeoning friendship between the two leaders could not hide the fact that the people of East Timor were getting frustrated.

After several months, the UN-led administration had been unable to reduce poverty, rebuild the economic infrastructure, or create the conditions to receive the 300,000 refugees trying to return to their country. In addition, East Timorese feared a resurgence of Indonesian occupation.

In that context, Sérgio attended a major gathering of the resistance movement to acknowledge their concerns: "We hear clearly your concerns that [the UN mission] fails to communicate or involve East Timorese sufficiently." He explained that the security and economic situation was extremely fragile and everyone needed to work together to face the challenges. He wanted locals to take an active part in shaping the future of East Timor and offered two models: "Under the first model, [the UN mission] and myself will continue to be the punching bag," he quipped. And under the second model they could have a "co-government" that would speed up the transition to full independence.

"This was the time we were convinced that Sérgio was committed to the Timorese," Xanana recalls. "The Security Council had given him all of the powers, but he said, 'No, I need you.'"

To deliver on his promise of co-government, Sérgio formed a national council led by local leaders, including Xanana. He created a cabinet in which half of the top positions were filled with East Timorese. And he established a judiciary system composed of East Timorese judges and prosecutors. In just over two years, the co-government model cultivated security and stability, and established the basis for democracy and economic growth. On April 24, 2002, the people of East Timor elected Xanana Gusmão as their first president.

After his time in East Timor, Sérgio served as the UN High Commissioner for Human Rights, and, later, the UN Special Representative in Iraq. It was in that role that he was killed in the attack on the UN headquarters in Baghdad on August 19, 2003.

Coincidentally, the following day, about 20,000 East Timorese had congregated outside of Dili to honor those who had died in the war for independence. Xanana had watched footage of the UN attack on TV, and when it was his turn to speak, he told the group that Sérgio had been killed by a bomb. The attendees were visibly shaken. When it was time to read the names of martyred East Timorese, the Bishop included the name *Sérgio Vieira de Mello*.

I first heard Sérgio's story when I was at university. I was struck by how he engaged with others to gain their trust and work together. Sérgio could have just followed the Security Council resolution that said that the UN alone was responsible for governing. But he was not afraid of sharing power. He used his personal narrative to build empathy and foster trust with local leaders. He created a sense of common purpose, inviting them to join the government.

For more than 15 years, I have been fortunate to work with talented leaders and high-performing professionals in international development, business, finance, and the nonprofit sector. The most successful have something in common: like Sérgio, they are expert communicators and relationship builders. They have clarity of purpose and a deep understanding of their goals and ambitions. They project their true selves for all to see. And while each has a unique style for getting the job done, they all rely on narratives and stories to engage and motivate others.

Humans are hardwired to learn through storytelling. Stories help us make sense of complex information and retain what we've learned. Stories also appeal to our emotions, which often compel us to commit to a mission or cause.

Further, stories can be used to create collective narratives, which are essential for humans to work with each other in large numbers. Yuval Noah Harari, a historian from the Hebrew University of Jerusalem, explains that humans can cooperate flexibly with countless numbers of strangers because we alone can create and believe narratives. As long as everyone follows the same narrative (with underlying norms, values, and rules), we can exist cooperatively side by side.

"We humans control the world because we live in a dual reality. All other animals live in an objective reality. Their reality consists of objective entities, like rivers and trees and lions and elephants. We humans also live in an objective reality. In our world, too, there are rivers and trees and lions and elephants. But over the centuries, we have constructed on top of this objective reality a second layer of fictional reality, a reality made of fictional entities, like nations, like gods, like money, like corporations.

And what is amazing is that as history unfolded, this fictional reality became more and more powerful, so that today, the most powerful forces in the world are these fictional entities. Today, the very survival of rivers and trees and lions and elephants depends on the decisions and wishes of fictional entities, like the United States, like Google, like the World Bank—entities that exist only in our own imagination."[2]

Although Harari calls them "fictional," these entities are often the biggest and most important part of the reality we experience. And whether we're talking about the president of an entire country, the CEO of a Fortune 500 company, or even the local head of a grassroots volunteer network, leaders use narratives to facilitate cooperation or win others over for their organizations and causes. But creating narratives that resonate with others is challenging when so many competing messages demand our attention.

In January 2020, the MIT Sloan Management Review released a survey of top professionals from more than 120 countries about the skills needed for effective leadership in the decades ahead. The survey found that, even more than in the past, leaders will need to articulate a clear sense of purpose, vision, and strategy. In other words, they will have to shape a narrative.

"In the digital economy, physical presence can't be mandatory to be an effective leader. You have to be able to lead people from many different cultures, in many different locations, and often with imperfect information because things are moving so fast.... You have to be able to see a story emerging and to articulate that story in a way that has meaning and inspiration for a wide range of people. You have to convey your passion and beliefs through a powerful narrative."[3]—Susan Sobbott, former president of American Express Global Commercial Services

In my own experience, I have also seen first-hand how much listening effective leaders do. They make a conscious effort to get to know their team members, partners, and others they work with. They try to understand what others care about and what motivates them—and from there build a narrative that facilitates collaboration. They create an environment of trust and they empower others to take initiative and be their best.

Today, more than ever, professionals who want to achieve results need to be sharp in their approach to communicating and building relationships. People crave genuine communication and meaningful interactions that invite them to be part of something that matters.

In this book I articulate the Expanding Circle framework, which helps us understand how some of the most effective leaders and professionals communicate and engage with others successfully. I also share some stories to illustrate the framework and discuss other important traits of leadership communication and relationship building. Many of the stories feature former or current clients, but I also include stories of other leaders I know and admire. I was able to interview all of these people for the book and thank all of them for their time and generosity.

THE EXPANDING CIRCLE FRAMEWORK

If I am not for myself, then who will be for me? And if I am only for myself, then what am I? And if not now, when?
—Rabbi Hillel

THE EXPANDING CIRCLE FRAMEWORK

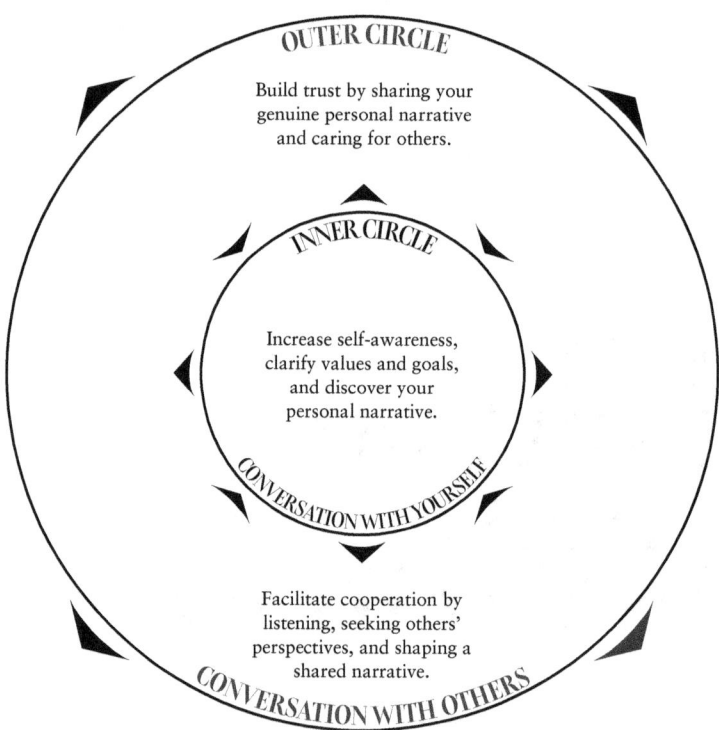

OUTER CIRCLE
Build trust by sharing your genuine personal narrative and caring for others.

INNER CIRCLE
Increase self-awareness, clarify values and goals, and discover your personal narrative.

CONVERSATION WITH YOURSELF

Facilitate cooperation by listening, seeking others' perspectives, and shaping a shared narrative.

CONVERSATION WITH OTHERS

When the inner and outer conversations are aligned and true connections are forged, the circles expand —and your influence grows.

THE NEED FOR GENUINE LEADERSHIP

We live in a time of constant change and pressing challenges. Think, for example, about climate change, widespread inequality, technological disruption, global social movements. These trends represent both wicked problems and heady challenges that call for a special kind of leadership.

Broadly speaking, we can differentiate between leading by formal authority or by influence. A leader who relies on his formal authority has the power or right to give orders, make decisions, and enforce compliance. People do as he says, not because they believe in the approach, but because they have no other option. The authoritative leader must dictate every aspect of what he wants his followers to do—and manage how and when they do it. All of which is impossible in organizations that need to quickly adapt to the demands of a digital economy, where specialization and continuous innovation are critical, and where many organizations are increasingly decentralized.

In contrast, leading by influence means working with others so they are motivated to follow a course of action, not just because they are told to do so, but because they believe in it. This kind of leader listens, molds consensus, and sets a strategic direction. She does not micromanage every aspect of what others do. Rather, she empowers followers to take ownership of initiatives that are important to them and become leaders themselves, while contributing to the broader organizational goals. Given the right motivation, people go out of their way to proactively address urgent and complex challenges.

How does one lead by influence and not just authority? What makes people connect to leaders and want to follow them? Embracing a genuine leadership style is one approach that not only works, but is broadly accessible. It does not require any specific innate characteristics (charisma or intuitive powers, for example), but instead can be achieved with practice.

Genuine leaders follow their inner convictions and passions, and engage with others in an authentic and open way. They have a deep understanding of themselves, and at the same time lead with generosity. They care about others and empower others to fulfill their own ambitions. These leaders show you who they are as human beings, rather than hiding behind a mantle of power. They are not afraid to share their personal stories and connect those stories to collective narratives that foster trust and a sense of shared purpose—helping others find meaning in their own lives.[4]

The need for purpose is even more important as leaders engage with Millennials and Generation Z in the workforce. These generations crave purpose as well as high ethical standards from their employers. Just think about the 32,000 students in France that signed a pledge to work for environmentally conscious companies, or the thousands of Google employees that signed a letter protesting the company's involvement in a Pentagon program that uses artificial intelligence to enhance the targeting of drone strikes.

These generations also want autonomy and empowerment. They look for environments where they can decide how the job gets done. A recent Gallup study of the American workforce finds that 42 percent of Millennials would switch to a job that allows them to work independently on a project of their choosing, and 63 percent to a job that allows them flextime.[5]

When people work alongside genuine leaders, they often give their whole hearts and minds to the mission. They feel motivated to work with others, to innovate, and try to produce extraordinary results. In other words, genuine leaders are well positioned to make a difference in a world that calls for complex collaboration and innovation.

Genuine leadership can be learned and developed by working consciously to increase self-awareness and build meaningful connections. It can also be exercised at any stage in your professional journey. In this book, you will find case studies of seasoned leaders, but also of young, emerging ones. At its most basic level, genuine leadership is about knowing yourself and being able to mobilize a group of people toward a common goal. There is no universal formula or checklist for genuine leadership. Every leader has to find what is genuine for himself or herself, reflecting the leader's true values and convictions. The Expanding Circle framework can help us get there.

COMMUNICATING AND BUILDING RELATIONSHIPS

Communication and relationship building are essential for genuine leadership. Think about a person creating an interdisciplinary team, running a complex project, or even just building a strong professional network. When connection leads to cooperation, we see impact. And when that impact leads to more connection and more cooperation, our influence grows. Honing our ability to engage authentically with ourselves and those around us is key to growing as a leader. And when we consider how our growth and influence can be multiplied by a continuous and dynamic cycle of self-reflection, conversation, and relationship building, we begin to embody the leader we could be. This is the Expanding Circle.

In the following pages, I will deconstruct the Expanding Circle framework into its two parts: the inner circle and the outer circle. This will help us understand how the framework functions so you can begin to use it as a tool to plan your own communication and engagement strategy.

We will start with the inner circle. This is the conversation you have with yourself—which can be more or less conscious. It's how you gain self-awareness, connect with your desires and ambitions, and set your goals. Internal awareness allows you to lead from a place of authenticity, rather than conforming to others' expectations. Trying to cater to others, without regard for what you feel and value, is emotionally consuming and not very effective; others will realize that you are not being genuine. Being true to your inner convictions also allows you to communicate with confidence and show your passion.

We will then move onto the outer circle—the relationships you build with others. Here, it is crucial to communicate from the outcome of your inner conversation. This will help you gain clarity of purpose—having a sharp understanding of why you are approaching another person and what you would like that person to do. We also need to direct our focus to the other, and seek out the person's perspective. We do this not by assuming or trying to imagine what someone is thinking, but by doing the work of deep listening. We have our own inner circle; others have theirs. We need to be able to engage in a manner that resonates with them.

When the inner and outer circles are aligned, you begin to connect with others in a genuine way. You help others and allow others to help you. Networks are strengthened and your message becomes louder. In other words, your influence expands.

Done well, the Expanding Circle framework is a complement and reinforcer of a strategy. You might have the best business idea or policy solution. However, if you have trouble describing it and fail to get the support from the right people, your idea will flounder. The opposite is also true. You can foster a deep connection with the people you need to support your business or public policy idea. They might believe in you as a leader and want to collaborate with you. However, if the idea is flawed, sooner or later they will stop supporting you.

But even in cases of "failure," fostering true connections pays off. If people perceive you as a genuine leader, that you truly care about them and have their best interest in mind, they might just give you a second chance. That is the beauty of the Expanding

Circle—it's about much more than that single team, project, or network. People crave meaningful communication and relationships, and are increasingly aware of the value of genuine collaboration to make a difference. Committing to these principles may be a life-long endeavor, but the rewards are reaped over a lifetime.

THE INNER CIRCLE

If we have our own "why" of life we shall get along with almost any "how."
—Friedrich Nietzsche

THE EXPANDING CIRCLE
INNER CIRCLE

When the inner and outer conversations are aligned
and true connections are forged, the circles expand
—and your influence grows.

DEFINING YOUR VALUES, AMBITIONS AND GOALS

Think of your inner circle as a dynamic conversation with yourself—a space to connect (and reconnect) with your true values, ambitions, and goals. Connecting with yourself is essential to growing, developing an integrated self, and finding meaning about who you are and purpose for what you do. That purpose might change over time as you grow as a person and professional—and that's a good thing. When the inner conversation is honest, we find harmony and clarity. This gives us the confidence to engage authentically with others. For seasoned leaders—who have a solid grasp on these core principles—an occasional check-in on the inner circle can be helpful. For emerging leaders or professionals seeking a career change, it's absolutely imperative.

The first step is focused self-reflection. I have seen leaders and high-achieving professionals approach this exercise in different ways. Everyone will need to determine what works best for them. However, I have found the following pointers helpful to begin the process:

o Find quiet time to connect with yourself and reflect. There are many ways of doing this, including coaching, meditation, long walks, journaling, etc.

o Explore your life stories and identify situations where you had to make difficult choices.
  o What do you identify in yourself in that situation that you would like to keep or develop further as you move forward? What would you like to put behind you?

o Ask yourself the following:

o What values do you consider important? Are you living your values right now? If not, what's holding you back?

o What is the one cause or issue you deeply care about and would like to focus on? Why is it important to you?

o What goals would you like to set for yourself that are aligned with your values? What would you like to achieve in the next one, three, and five years?

o Imagine you are writing your memoir. What would be the title of the book and what would be the title of the last chapter? (Try coming up with titles for several more chapters leading to the last one.)

o Craft your professional mission statement. Write out a short paragraph that describes who you are and what your mission is.

Exploring your values, ambitions, and goals—and more generally your inner circle—is a deeply personal process, but cannot be done in isolation. Test your ideas in the real world, see how others react, and notice what you feel when faced with those reactions.

Committing to this process doesn't have to mean that everything changes overnight. You can start small. Try choosing a project you are already leading and commit to approaching it through the lenses of the values and goals you have identified. If you said in your mission statement that you want to "empower others," let team members take initiative; don't micromanage. If you want to work on a cause you care deeply about, share with your team why it is so important to you. Throughout the project, seek honest feedback from colleagues, friends, mentors, bosses, partners, or team members. It is important to truly listen and acknowledge what others are telling you. Talking only to those who will tell you what you want to hear is not going to help you grow.

Over time, this dynamic process of self-reflection will become more natural. You will be able to lead bigger initiatives, shaping them and connecting with others in harmony with what you care about and who you are as a person. You will be able to create a feedback loop between your inner circle and your connection with others—a dialectic dynamic in which one enriches the other. And remember, regular check-ins are important. Some of the most seasoned leaders I have worked with take days off from the office every six months to connect with themselves and reflect on their inner circle. In the following pages, we'll learn about Diego Bekerman, a Microsoft executive who has built a successful career by owning up to his mistakes—and learning from them.

LEARNING FROM MISTAKES
THE CASE OF DIEGO

Diego Bekerman says that he can't pinpoint one event that made him the leader he is today. But looking closely at two crises—ten years apart—helps us understand his evolution as a leader.

Diego is the General Manager for Small, Medium and Corporate Customers of Microsoft in Latin America and the Caribbean. Talking to him, you immediately sense his passion for his work, and his belief in the promise of new technologies to spread knowledge and create a more inclusive society. "Voy con todo y por todo," he says. "Put all of yourself into anything you decide to do and try to achieve as much as possible."

Along with his passion and determination, Diego has extraordinary focus—doggedly working toward strategic, long-term goals despite adversity and failure. At the same time, he makes a conscious effort to be self-aware, take feedback seriously, and work on his weaknesses—which helps him learn from setbacks and rebound stronger.

He is widely respected in the business community, with that rare talent for taking complex technology issues and making them relevant for lay audiences. Whether talking to public officials, business owners, or high-school students, Diego uses stories that resonate with his audience, helping them appreciate the possibilities that technology can bring to their lives. In a recent conference with retailers, for instance, Diego talked about the transition from horses to automobiles as an analogy for the current transformation of the digital economy. The automobile revolution brought turmoil, but also possibility; the same is happening with the digital economy.

At Microsoft, Diego is a trusted and admired leader, making sure he creates the space for others to share their ideas and get involved. He is also keen on open communication with his team. He believes that it is important to foster a shared narrative with a clear purpose to bring the team together, especially in difficult times.

He also understands that, especially in competitive corporate environments such as Microsoft, people have their own professional goals. Therefore, he told me, he looks for people with the ability to align their personal goals with those of the team. At the same time, it's important that managers create incentives, such as bonuses or public recognition, that encourage employees to contribute to the shared purpose. In that sense, Diego shapes the team's shared narrative not only with words and stories, but also with concrete actions.

Finally, when Diego realizes he has made a mistake, he has the courage to openly recognize it and take steps to make it right. This helps him foster trust with his employees.

But this wasn't always the case.

In 2008, Diego, just 33 at the time, was named director for small- and medium-sized companies at Microsoft in Argentina. "It was a dream come true," Diego recalls. Yet, that promotion coincided with a worldwide market collapse. Lehman Brothers had shut down. Goldman Sachs was barely holding on. No one knew what to do in this rapidly changing and uncertain environment.

Against all odds, Diego found a way for his team to succeed. "At that time, we decided to offer a co-investment model to provide small and medium businesses with much-needed financing. It was different from anything else available. The model became successful in a period in which the market was flat or stagnant. We reached a growth model that allowed us to double our business in a year," Diego explains.

With his winning strategy, Diego received recognition from Microsoft's management at the regional and global levels: "We received awards, recognitions....We were invited to present at global corporate conferences," he says.

But the market conditions began to change, damaging the performance of his business accounts. "Even when we saw the market variables were changing, we did not read them correctly. We were blinded by the success we had obtained. By the time we realized that the model was hitting its own limits, it was too late," Diego remembers.

Diego and his team never managed to recalibrate their business model. However, as Diego later realized, that was not his main failure. Diego had responded to the crisis by questioning other people's decisions and reorganizing teams. "When the model started to fail us, the first thing we did was start looking for people to blame instead of analyzing if we had reacted well to the changing circumstances."

At this point, other managers may have doubled down or simply moved on, confident that past successes would protect them. Not Diego. "Sometimes you look for someone to hold responsible without looking at the whole picture, and without first looking at yourself," Diego reflects. "On a personal level, this experience brought me humility, and I recognized that nothing is forever, and that the path of continuous learning is the one that brings better fruits and better return." He also worked to make amends with those he had hurt: "I could have just moved on, but I needed to talk to others—including many who had been impacted by my decisions—to fully appreciate what I had done wrong."

For Diego, learning from errors is key to growth. "To become a better leader, you need to question yourself, look deeper, and become more aware of the full context to be able to adjust on the fly. Nothing is sustainable forever. As a leader, you need to know how to read and anticipate roadblocks and change course. And, above all, put the team and the impact first. Even before you."

A decade later, Diego's leadership skills would be tested again.

In 2019, Argentina held presidential elections that would—overnight—turn the environment for doing business upside down. For four years, the country had had a business-friendly government, led by the Cambiemos political coalition. While this administration had failed to deliver much good to the majority of the population, few thought that the more populist Peronist party (which had ended their previous administration with a poor economy and numerous accusations of corruption) would prevail in the elections. They were wrong. The Peronist party won the election.[6] In a sign of the economic turbulence that would follow, the Argentine peso devalued by more than 30 percent the day after the Peronist party won.

At the time, Diego was in his fourth year as the director general of Microsoft in Argentina. Over the years, he had fostered good relationships within the Cambiemos administration and had developed a business model that responded to a business-friendly environment. The results of the elections had an immediate impact on the business strategy but also on the people of Diego's team.

Their salaries had just significantly devalued. Staff members were not sure how the company would continue to perform and therefore what their prospects for career advancement would be. Anxiety levels were skyrocketing.

It would have been easy to simply blame the situation; virtually no political analyst had anticipated the election results. But Diego's response was different from the one he had a decade previously. He had learned his lesson.

He gathered his leadership team and agreed on how they would deal with the situation. Then, he organized a town hall to talk to staff. Diego acknowledged that the situation took him by surprise. "I did not see it coming," Diego shared. "But we are well positioned to adjust and face this situation."

Diego and his leadership team worked together to be more proactive and adjust the business model as needed. "Every Monday, I meet with the leadership team and plan for all potential scenarios." He also instituted an open-door policy for staff that wanted to share ideas or discuss any personal concerns given the economic uncertainty. "I wanted people to know that we had their backs, that if we delivered the minimum we needed to—given the turbulent context—the organization would back us."

Importantly, Diego used the situation to reaffirm the team's common purpose. At the town hall, with small groups, and in one-on-one meetings, he reminded employees that they needed to stay focused and remember their team vision: to facilitate the use of technology in the region to create a more inclusive society. Then, they needed to focus on what they had to do to adjust their operations and deliver. Above all, they needed to focus on clients and how to support them.

In the months following the crisis, Diego's team adjusted and adapted—and continued to deliver for the company. Trust was deepened; sense of purpose swelled. And Diego was ready to face his next challenge—whatever that may be.

KEY TAKEAWAYS

○ Connecting with your inner circle in an honest way helps you find harmony and clarity about who you are and what you care about. Over the years, Diego has made a conscious effort to increase his self-awareness, understand his strengths, and learn from his mistakes. This gave him confidence to engage authentically with others.

○ Showing your authentic self fosters trust with others. Diego has learned to be open with his team—showing himself as an ambitious and results-driven leader, but also as a person who cares about others and is not afraid to acknowledge his mistakes. Genuine communication helps Diego build trust with his staff, creating the conditions for people to contribute their best and deliver for the team.

DEVELOPING YOUR PERSONAL NARRATIVE

Once you have defined your values, ambitions, and goals, it is time to develop a personal narrative—how you want to position yourself when you engage with others. A genuine personal narrative stems directly from our inner circle, drawing on who we are as professionals and as human beings. It engenders trust and signals to others how they can work with us to pursue a meaningful goal.

Articulating our personal narrative and then sharing it with others also provides meaning for ourselves. It reminds us of who we are and what we care about. When a personal narrative reflects our true self, it helps us stay in harmony with our inner circle. When it doesn't, it drains our emotional energy as we try to embody a narrative that does not show who we really are.

We've all seen talented young professionals choosing a career because of the promise of prestige or salary, or executives sacrificing close relationships or time with loved ones to quickly scale the corporate ladder and make more money. They probably tell stories to themselves—and to others—to convince themselves that they are pursuing something meaningful and fulfilling. But inside they know that what they are doing is not aligned with their values and true ambitions.

The good news is that people can rid themselves of false narratives—of the ideas that don't reflect who they really are and are not helpful in developing a fulfilling life and career. Going through the exercises in the previous section, as well as the process to articulate a narrative we will review next, can help us craft a narrative that reflects our inner self.

Often, "narrative" and "story" are used as synonyms. For the purpose of this book, I will use "narrative" to describe a way of looking at the world—an overarching concept that influences thought, meaning, and decision-making. Narrative gives meaning to a broader vision, a view of what's possible, and why we should head in that direction. In contrast, a story recounts a series of moments, tied to specific times and places. It has a beginning, middle, and end, and explores the desires, dilemmas, and choices that people face. A story can provide us with an insight or even a lesson, and create a shared emotional experience for the storyteller and the audience.

Think of a story as an individual scene and the narrative as the movie. The narrative is what connects the dots. A good narrative will use a range of stories to illustrate, animate, and validate its message. Powerful personal narratives consist of three elements: what, how, and why.[7]

○ **What.** This is a plain description of the product of your work. For instance, you could say: "I am a finance professional and focus on affordable housing" or "I am a doctor and help cure people."

○ **How.** This adds detail about the way you approach your work. For example, you could explain: "I am a finance professional and structure financial products to help low-income families buy a home" or "I am a doctor who works long hours and is always available for my patients on the phone."

○ **Why.** This explains what ultimately motivates you to do what you do. For instance, you could say: "I care about creating opportunities for low-income families, and affordable housing allows these families to have more money for health and education for their children" or "I care about helping people be healthy, so they can live life to the fullest."

Most people are good at communicating what they do. Many people have clarity about how they do what they do. But it is rarer to find people who know why they do what they do. Those are the people who understand what moves them—or in other words, who have clarity on their inner circle. Later, we'll get to know Rachel Kyte, the unconventional dean of the Fletcher School of Law and Diplomacy. Rachel's story is one of deep self-reflection and hard work to align her personal values with a leadership role—and about the story she told to connect with others.

When we talk about the what or the how, we are communicating at the rational level. If you said, "I produce inexpensive shoes that are made of all-natural materials," you might persuade a potential customer to buy a pair of shoes, but you likely won't create a loyal brand follower. Or think about a young professional who has joined your company to gain industry experience and start paying off her student loans. The minute she gets an offer for more money, she will probably leave.

The why, however, is tied to values and emotions. It provides a deeper meaning to what you do and motivates you to do it better. It also helps others understand why you do what you do, giving them a glimpse of the real you. This helps foster deeper cooperation and collaboration—others will want to share in that feeling of purpose. Thinking about the examples above, the why might be as simple as, "I take pride in making affordable, high-quality products that don't harm the environment," or "I foster a workplace that supports employees and encourages their growth."

I encourage you to go through the what, how, and why exercise, focusing primarily on the why. This will help you clarify your inner motivations, which will then lay the foundation for your personal narrative. Only then should we begin to choose the specific stories that will bring that narrative to life.

STORIES TO SUPPORT YOUR PERSONAL NARRATIVE

You have more than one genuine and true story in you. Think about challenges you have faced, important choices you have made, and outcomes you have experienced. How have these experiences shaped and defined you? And what is the "learning" from these experiences—what is the main lesson or message you would like to convey to others? The following questions can help you find your story:

o **Challenge.** Why did you consider it a challenge? What in particular made it so challenging? What about who you are as a person made it your challenge?

o **Choice.** What options did you have to address this challenge? How did you come to the choice you made? Did it take courage or hope to get there, and if so, why were you able to access those parts of you at that moment? How did you feel when you made the choice? What actions did you take to follow through?

○ **Outcome.** Was this the expected outcome? How did you feel about the outcome? Why did it make you feel that way?

○ **Learning.** What have you learned? What would you like others to remember as the main message of your story? How would you like others to feel when they remember your story?

Try to get as vivid as possible as you craft your story. Do not be afraid of connecting with the emotions you had when you faced the challenge you are describing. That will help others connect with your story at a deeper level. Once you have identified your stories, you can start to weave them into your personal narrative, recognizing that, depending on the specific circumstances and audience, you will likely use different stories to support the same narrative.

Ultimately, stories are a powerful tool to convey big ideas and connect with others. However, even leaders that feel comfortable using stories to shape a collective narrative—a narrative that articulates what a group does and why—sometimes balk at the idea of using their personal stories to articulate an individual narrative. But as we will see in some of the following case studies, narratives are also shaped by actions. In fact, there should be alignment between the leader's stories and actions—what the person says and does. Some leaders, even without explicitly using their personal stories, are able to create a personal narrative based on their actions.

A WINDOW TO CONNECT
THE CASE OF RACHEL

The Fletcher School of Law and Diplomacy is a prestigious institution—and a very traditional one. It first accepted students in the fall of 1933 as a partnership between Harvard and Tufts—becoming the first graduate-only school of international affairs. Over the years, Fletcher has earned a reputation for successfully preparing students for the United States Foreign Service, hosting military scholars, and conceiving some of the most influential ideas in the field of international relations. Despite these strengths, the board of trustees felt that Fletcher was in need of modernization. They wanted a leader who would propel the school to the vanguard of the 21st century. They chose Rachel Kyte, the first woman to ever hold the position.

Rachel is a rather unconventional choice to lead an academic institution, however. Originally from a working-class area of Eastern England, she began her career as a social and environmental activist. And as she told me, "once you become an activist, you are always an activist." She eventually made her way to Fletcher where she graduated from the Global Master of Arts Program in 2002. But she did not pursue a doctorate or a career in research. Instead, she became a practitioner of international development.

Holding high-ranking positions at the United Nations, the World Bank, and the International Finance Corporation, Rachel has dedicated her career to tackling global issues like poverty, clean and affordable energy, and climate change. Over time, she has gained a reputation as a changemaker pushing organizations from within to become more transparent, inclusive, and closer to the people they serve in the developing world. "Rachel's leadership and commitment to addressing global challenges ... combined with her deep understanding of the complexities of multilateral international negotiations, and her advocacy for the marginalized in society—make her the perfect choice to lead The Fletcher School," noted Tufts President Anthony P. Monaco.[8]

For Rachel, the position at Fletcher represented both an opportunity to help shape the next generation of leaders, and a chance to recommit more time and energy to her wife, Ilyse, and her two children. In short, the job would help her align her inner and outer circles. "I feel very strongly that this world has to be better for [my children].... It's not fair to hand things off the way things currently are. My son is fourteen, my daughter is eleven. I've got work to do to till the ground for them."[9]

She envisioned a new path for Fletcher—one that would represent a break from aspects of the school's history and reputation. "Our own narrative is getting in the way of who we could be," she explained. They needed to create a place where people from all over the world could come together around the most pressing global issues of our lifetimes—such as inequality, climate change, and sustainable growth.

To do so, they needed to create a more diverse and inclusive place—welcoming to seasoned military scholars, first-generation college students, the LGBTQIA community, and everyone in between. They needed to diversify the faculty and to accept more international students from middle- and low-income families. For that they would need to drastically change the financing model, increase donations, grow their endowment, and be creative in finding new sources of income. "If the tuition is $40,000 and we give a $20,000 grant, that's still impossible for most people in the developing world."[10]

As a seasoned communicator, Rachel knew she needed to lead this transformation with her personal narrative. She understood that many people in the Fletcher family—board members, faculty, students, parents, donors—did not know her well. She needed to create a window to connect with people. "If they see me, see what moves me and what helps me be a better person, what I believe, what I have done and want to do, they have something to hold on to," she told me.

From the beginning, Rachel opened up about herself and her narrative—making sure to be true to herself no matter who she was speaking to. "Whether I'm talking to the academic dean, the president, the head of the student council, one of the administrative staff, or the cleaners, there's only one Rachel Kyte, dean of Fletcher." She spoke about her passions, her fears, and her personal and professional commitment to being courageous. This set the tone for her leadership style and for what she knew would be a difficult transformation ahead.

> "I've gotten into cars with a blindfold on to go and negotiate. I have been arrested at roadblocks trying to do my job. I have run into a doorway as the police tried to quell a protest. Those are the traditionally sort of 'dangerous' things that diplomats or officials or young politicians have done. We need people who are courageous and prepared to do those things to pursue a common good.... But standing up as a minority and saying who you are and what you believe also feels dangerous, and sometimes is dangerous. This is a kind of danger and courage duopoly that I want the students of Fletcher to explore. As a lesbian, it has been an interesting journey of having to come out, sometimes every day. It takes courage to be the person who stands up and says, 'No, this is who I am,' to not just let something go. If I can help keep the door open, if I can create the space for people to be themselves, I'll be very proud."[11]

After using her personal narrative to draw people in, she started to foster a collective narrative for the Fletcher community that would help create a common purpose and direction. And that involved a lot of listening. She talked to everyone—professors, students, board members, donors, alumni. She needed allies to help shape her long-term vision for the school and convert it into an actionable plan. "I work with the 80/20 rule," Rachel told me, meaning if she can get 80 percent of the people to support her, she can succeed. As for that other 20 percent: "You listen to them, try to connect where you can, and then make it clear that you are as tough as they are."

After just five months on the job, Rachel had gained a lot of support. As one student told me: "It was inspiring and refreshing listening to her. She would be very open and update us on what she was doing to bring organizations with big global issues looking for help so students, together with professors, could be part of the solution."

But in the spring of 2020, COVID-19 stopped everything in its tracks.

Within a few weeks, the school had stopped all in-person classes and moved its courses online. Many students packed up and returned home. Newly vacant portions of the campus were converted into temporary hospital facilities and housing for quarantined individuals.

But some courses were more difficult than others to migrate online, and some professors were more tech savvy and inclined to talk to a camera than others. Some parents had lost their jobs or had their incomes cut, and were concerned about how to pay their child's tuition. Students were concerned about what would happen with their planned internships or whether they could find jobs after graduation.

As I write this, we are still in the middle of the pandemic, so it is not possible to fully assess how effective Rachel has been at leading the school through the crisis. But Rachel understands that clear and consistent communication is key. Through live-streaming messages, emails, video chats, phone conversations, and tweets, she is keeping lines of communication open, showing how school leadership is doing its best to be proactive and thorough.

She keeps her communications real and human—she is the dean, but she is also communicating as Rachel, the person. Sometimes, she shares when she has a bad day or what she is doing to cope with the stay-at-home orders—including readings and her lockdown playlist. "I am trying to give them permission to have bad days, feel anxious."

Particularly with students, she tries to use the situation as a teachable moment. "I had one student write to me asking for help with an internship, reminding me that I had promised him I would talk to this company but he had not heard from them ... and I said, 'Wait, wait, wait ... I am going to help you' but they might be struggling with their own issues. We need to be patient and try to understand each other."

The bond Rachel created with the school community before COVID-19 has helped her connect with students, faculty, and community members during the pandemic—helping them feel reassured that she cares and is doing her best to handle the situation. As one student told me, she does not know whether she will be able to graduate on time and find a job. She feels frustrated after years of studying hard and the financial effort her parents have made. But "having somebody like Rachel, somebody with a lot of experience, somebody you can talk to, somebody who cares, makes all the difference."

Rachel has achieved this bond with her community by having a deep understanding of who she is and what she stands for. She has not been afraid to share that narrative—her inner circle—with others. And by being transparent about her vision for the future of the school and encouraging others to help shape the change, she is creating a new generation of honest and courageous leaders. That, she believes, is the best way to honor the school tradition.

KEY TAKEAWAYS

○ By taking the position as the dean of Fletcher, Rachel aligned her inner and outer circles, helping her to lead with purpose. She recommitted to her family and engaged with the school's community to foster a new generation of leaders to address the most pressing global issues—problems that she believes need to be tackled to leave her children a better world.

○ Leading with your genuine personal narrative is a powerful tool to create trust and connect with others. Sharing her personal narrative allowed Rachel to connect with the Fletcher community quickly. She was not afraid to be open and show her true self, creating a window to connect with people and foster the trust needed to transform the school. This connection also positions her well to lead the school through the COVID-19 crisis.

THE OUTER CIRCLE

When people talk, listen completely. Most people never listen.
—Ernest Hemingway

When we come together to do important things, it's usually because we told a good story about why we should be working together.
—Barack Obama

THE EXPANDING CIRCLE
OUTER CIRCLE

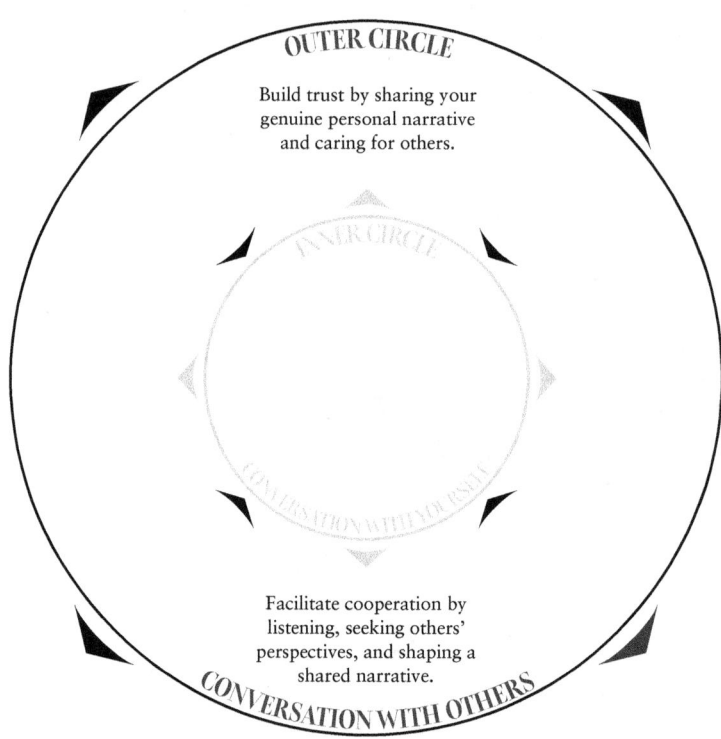

When the inner and outer conversations are aligned
and true connections are forged, the circles expand
—and your influence grows.

MEANINGFUL CONNECTIONS

The outer circle is your opportunity to establish genuine, two-way connections with others—colleagues, friends, business partners, mentors, etc. This is not the meet-and-greet, transactional networking you may be used to. Relating to others in a transactional way rarely helps you collaborate with others to foster meaningful changes or deliver breakthrough results. The connections you build and maintain in your outer circle are rooted in empathy, mutual understanding, and a desire to work together toward a common goal. A rich outer circle helps you find meaning and joy in your career—and in life.

To truly connect with others, you must be able to see things from their perspective. Dale Carnegie, in his classic *How to Win Friends and Influence People*, argues that one of the secrets of success lies in the ability to see things from others' points of view as well as from your own.

Many people rely on past experiences or even "intuition" to guess what others want. But intuition is a shortcut—and not a particularly good one. Several studies have shown that most people are pretty terrible at guessing others' perspectives.[12] Emily Pronin, from Princeton University, goes even further and argues that there is a tendency to believe that others do not know us, but that we know others.

> "The conviction that we know others better than they know us—and that we may have insights about them they lack (but not vice versa)—leads us to talk when we would do well to listen and to be less patient than we ought to be when others express the conviction that they are the ones who are being misunderstood or judged unfairly."[13]

Genuine leaders avoid prejudging others and truly listen to them, which allows them to really see the people they are trying to reach—who they are, what they care about, and what their goals are. Based on this deep understanding of others, these leaders can develop a shared narrative that sets common goals and facilitates cooperation among multiple parties.

Fostering trust is another crucial factor in establishing meaningful relationships. We have already discussed how a genuine personal narrative helps create that trust. But building strong relationships based on trust also takes time. Don't expect someone to immediately trust you simply because you opened yourself up to them. You must get to know and understand the person, and show him or her with actions that you care. Later, you'll read about Avi Hofman and Frank Taverner, co-directors of a major division at the International Finance Corporation. For them, developing open, trusting relationships between themselves and with staff made the difference between a chaotic and stressful company reorganization and one that ultimately proved massively successful—a model for the rest of their organization.

Outer circle relationships also need continuous nurturing. Keith Ferrazzi, in his book *Never Eat Alone and Other Secrets of Success*, argues that a relationship is like a muscle—the more you use it, the stronger it gets. But if you never exercise it, it might not respond when you need it. When I think about leaders and other professionals who have made a difference in their careers, I'm always struck by how much time they have invested in getting to know others.

Finally, it shouldn't come as a surprise that you need to genuinely care about other people to create lasting relationships. Showing interest in their lives, celebrating their strengths, helping them succeed—these are what drive meaningful connections. Flattery, insincerity, and competition have no place here. People will see right through you. As Carnegie explained:

"The difference between appreciation and flattery? That is simple. One is sincere and the other insincere. One comes from the heart out; the other from the teeth out. One is unselfish; the other selfish. One is universally admired; the other universally condemned.... If we stop thinking about ourselves for a while and begin to think of the other person's good points, we won't have to resort to flattery so cheap and false that it can be spotted almost before it is out of the mouth. So the only way on earth to influence other people is to talk about what they want and show them how to get it." [14]

Sérgio Vieira de Mello, the UN diplomat we discussed earlier, is a good example of this:

"Sérgio would talk to everybody—the security guard, a refugee, or a head of state ... and would pay real attention to them—trying to understand them—and would speak in terms that were relevant for them. Sérgio would also try to make others look good, not to hurt their egos, even if he disagreed with a person. For instance, Sérgio would listen to a person and then he would rephrase what the person had just said in a more articulate way...the person would feel flattered. You could argue that it was manipulation, but it was not. Sérgio cared deeply about others, about their dignity, and others perceived it. If not, they would have felt that Sérgio was not being genuine. And Sérgio was a genuine human being."—Fabrizio Hochschild-Drummond (Sérgio's long-time collaborator and chief of staff in East Timor).

UNDERSTANDING OTHERS

As we did with the inner circle, here are some pointers to help you start thinking about your outer circle. The questions below require that you engage in a conversation with others and truly listen to them. Try not to assume or prejudge. Go in with an open mind and take the time to get to know them.

○ Who are you trying to connect with?

○ What stories are they sharing with you? What else would you like to know about them?

○ What motivates them? What are their values? What do they care about?

○ What do you want them to do?
  ○ Think about specific behaviors (e.g., donate money, serve on a focus group, join your team).

○ What in your personal narrative would resonate with them and why?

○ What would be a collective narrative that resonates with them?
  ○ Think about shared values, experiences, and challenges.

○ What stories can you share with them to support that narrative?
  ○ Think about past experiences and challenges you may face in the future. These can be shared situations or not; just make sure that the messages are relevant for them and support the narrative you are trying to shape.

BUILDING RELATIONSHIPS
WITH THE RIGHT MINDSET

I t took me some time to understand the real value of relationships in building a rewarding and successful career—not to mention playing a leadership role and influencing others. I had the same mindset that I encounter in many young professionals. When faced with a rejection, I would say, "Another person got the job because the hiring manager really liked him." I put the blame on the other person instead of considering what it would take for others to like and care about me, and how I could help them.

In college, I was a sort of "perfect" student. I completed my political science degree with a near-perfect GPA and in record time. However, for a year, I could not get a job in my field.

In hindsight, I was too focused on me—on what I wanted to do (even though, in reality, I had no clear idea what that was). I was stuck in my head, scrolling job boards and listservs, searching for a "perfect" position working for this or that well-known person or prestigious organization. That's how I believed I would achieve success. But I never stopped to connect with people working for organizations I thought I would like to join, and try to actually understand what they needed—and, based on that, think about what I could offer. In other words, my inner conversation was bigger than my outer conversation. And my inner conversation wasn't honest. I was not genuinely connecting with my desires, values, ambitions, and goals.

That started to change when I decided to apply for a Fulbright scholarship to study abroad in the United States. After a year of rejections and missed opportunities, I was convinced I wouldn't get it. I had lots of reasons. Scholarships to study abroad were granted to students from elite private universities. Most of the professors who evaluated the applications taught at those universities; those kids had good connections. I had studied at a public school and did not know anybody. Qualified students usually had a very advanced level of English. At the time, my English was not very good. I was sure I would not qualify.

Nonetheless, I visited the Fulbright Commission office to learn about the requirements for the scholarship. While I was speaking with the receptionist, the director of the Commission, Norma Gonzalez, passed by and invited me to her office for a chat. She explained that the academic work was only one aspect of the program. The goal was really about improving and nurturing intercultural relations. They were looking for students who would go with an open mind, learn as much as possible, connect with other talented youth, and use that knowledge and those relationships to make a difference in their future careers.

They did not care whether applicants had attended private or public schools. In fact, they were interested in getting more applicants from public universities. The director also assured me that my English did not have to be perfect. She encouraged me to try to improve my level in the months before the application period started—she had seen it done in other cases and thought I could do it too.

I left the meeting having run out of reasons not to apply. I started spending three or more hours a day studying English, and began preparing my materials for the application. And then, just like that, I was in. I boarded a plane for Washington, DC to complete my master's degree in public management and communication.

When I got to DC, I literally did not know a single person. But I was in a new place, with a lot of amazing people to meet. It was the perfect opportunity to learn how to build a network. The Fulbright director had gone out of her way to counsel and guide me. But I could not expect everyone to do the same. Perhaps if I got out of my own head and was more curious about others, I could learn from them. If I connected with people in a different way, I might find people who could help me and (even more importantly) find opportunities to use my skills to help them. And I did it. I built a strong network of relationships that helped me find my way. I successfully completed my studies, landed a couple of dream internships, and secured a full-time job at a leading international development organization, where I built a rewarding career for more than ten years. Each and every step was possible thanks to the relationships I had cultivated.

My experience with the Fulbright director, and with many other generous people I have met since then, helped me realize I could trust others and engage with new people with an open mind. I felt I could share with them who I was and what my goals were—showing them who I was as a person and a professional. I was curious to learn about them, and as I learned more about others, I not only enriched myself with their stories and knowledge but also began to care about them. I connected with them in a genuine way. And my guess is that others noticed my sincere interest in them and valued it.

Engaging with others with the right mindset helps you build a meaningful outer circle. Be frank with yourself—and with others. Tell them where you are on your journey. More people than you think will appreciate your genuine approach and will want to help.

For me, one of those people was Fabian Koss, back then a senior executive at the Inter-American Development Bank who was in charge of running a network of hundreds of young leaders. I was looking for an internship to complement my academic studies and had heard that "he knew a lot of people," so I sent him an email. To my surprise, he responded promptly and invited me for coffee. I felt he was genuinely interested in learning about me, and he eventually hired me as part of his own team. With him, my education about how to connect with people in a meaningful way continued. In the next section, I tell his story.

BRIDGING OPPORTUNITIES
THE CASE OF FABIAN

I n 1994, Fabian Koss had just finished his master's degree in public affairs and was working at a small publishing house just outside of Washington, DC. While on a family vacation to Uruguay, he happened to meet Enrique V. Iglesias, then president of the Inter-American Development Bank (IDB), a financial institution dedicated to promoting social and economic progress in Latin America and the Caribbean. They struck up an easy conversation.

"Iglesias was like that—he would talk to an intern for a while and then turn around and have a conversation with a head of state," recalls Fabian, "I guess that's why he started talking to me."

Iglesias was curious about Fabian, wanting to know more about his background and career aspirations. After a lengthy conversation, he invited Fabian to join the IDB to organize a youth leadership summit to take place at the upcoming IDB board meeting in Jerusalem.

"I didn't know what I wanted to do professionally. I had been a fine student, but not an A-student. I was not an expert in anything. Iglesias somehow trusted me, believed in me, gave me an opportunity," Fabian explains. "At that time, the only credential I had to organize a youth conference was to be young myself. I was also a 'Latin-gringo' and Jewish, with some connections in Israel," he adds, referring to the fact that he had been born in Argentina, moved to the United States as a child, and had relatives and family friends in Israel. "You could argue that it was a case of positive profiling," he says, smiling.

Fabian wanted to explore his inner circle, but lacked clarity about his true calling. Through this opportunity, not only would he get to help others, he would also be able to shape his own inner conversation.

Fabian began traveling across Latin America and the Carib-bean, visiting universities as well as low-income neighborhoods—anywhere he might find young people taking initiative to improve the lives of others. Fabian tried to emulate Iglesias—talking to everyone, listening, and creating opportunities. Ultimately, he convened 150 young leaders at the IDB board meeting, many of whom had never been on an airplane before. "We gave them a seat at the table," Fabian recalls proudly.

The youth leadership conference was a success. Young leaders shared their work with each other, discussed common challenges, and found areas to collaborate. They also presented their work to IDB executives and board members. The senior management and government representatives already knew that youth were key for the development of Latin America and the Caribbean, where at that time more than half of the population was aged 24 and under. But now they realized that youth should play an active role in the solution. The summit led them to significantly increase the organization's financial support for young social entrepreneurs and youth development programs.

With the success of the summit under his belt, Fabian embarked on creating a regional network of young leaders that would receive ongoing support from the IDB. He wanted young leaders to shape their own network, since they knew better than anybody else what they needed to make a difference in their communities. Therefore, Fabian asked the summit participants to select a small group to work closely with him to start up the network.

Fabian would serve as the bridge back to the IDB. In this role, he began connecting network members to IDB economists and other specialists for technical assistance, and spent countless hours with representatives from governments, foundations, and private-sector companies to foster partnerships and secure funding for the network's projects.

Young leaders from all walks of life felt Fabian's genuine interest in them and wanted to work with him. Ambitious and idealistic young adults from universities in Latin America and the Caribbean (who often viewed the IDB and other multilateral finance institutions as remote and bureaucratic), perceived Fabian as a partner. Young leaders from slums who distrusted anyone wearing a suit also wanted to work with him. "I didn't invite them to be participants of an IDB program," Fabian explained. "I was asking them for me and the IDB to be part of their projects."

Fabian also found key allies within the IDB to ensure that large-scale projects at the bank included youth engagement. "Sometimes I was introduced as a youth specialist, but such a thing does not exist," he says. "Youth is a phase in a person's life, not an area of expertise." Supporting young people requires a multi-sectoral approach, including work in education, health, and infrastructure. Not an expert in any of those sectors, Fabian's job instead was to listen, understand, and connect. "I have always been a bridge; that's the value I bring."

Thanks to Fabian's work with the youth network, the IDB made it a priority to sponsor youth-oriented development projects across Latin America and the Caribbean. Some were rather traditional development projects—professional training centers for young people, for instance. But others were more unusual. In El Limon, a dangerous area in Guatemala ruled by gang warfare, Fabian's team partnered with a nonprofit, run by young local leaders, to offer free tattoo removal services to young people who wanted to remove gang-related ink. Without these tattoos, young people could start fresh, and seek out jobs and educational opportunities.

During one of his trips to Brazil, Fabian met Rodrigo Baggio, a young entrepreneur who had just founded the Committee for Democratization of Informatics (CDI). He and a team of volunteers would go to large businesses and ask for old computers about to be discarded. Committee volunteers would fix the computers and use them to teach programming and other digital skills to youth from slums and other low-income neighborhoods. In time, some of these young people would become instructors themselves.

Fabian connected Rodrigo and his team with IDB education experts to refine CDI's pedagogical approach. He also persuaded private technology companies, such as Microsoft, to help scale up their work to increase digital literacy—years before most international development funders even recognized the "digital divide" as a problem. With the IDB's support, CDI designed a business model and educational approach that was exported to other Latin American countries. To date, they have trained more than 100,000 young people.

As the IDB youth network continued to grow, Fabian explored new ways to promote the work of young leaders. In the late 1990s and early 2000s, MTV was the premier media outlet for adolescents and young adults. It had changed the music industry worldwide popularizing music videos. Fabian approached the Latin American branch of MTV and pitched an idea to share stories of real young people who were making a difference in the region.

The network was on board, but it would take a special team to turn this idea into reality. Mario Cader-Frech, a young Salvadorian in charge of creative teams at MTV, was just who Fabian needed. (He also happened to be a big believer in the power of social entrepreneurs.) Together, they created Agents of Change - Latin America. Fabian and his team found young leaders' stories to be featured and MTV donated millions of dollars in airtime and creative work. The show ultimately heightened the profile of the IDB youth network, helping Fabian attract new funding and foster new partnerships.

Fabian also made inroads using sports as a means to support youth development. In 2005, he created the A Ganar initiative, borrowing a common Spanish expression with a dual meaning: to win and to earn. The program used soccer to attract disadvantaged youth from slums and other low-income areas and teach them responsibility, teamwork, and communication. Vocational training helped participants also gain more practical skills to help them find employment or even start up their own businesses. Sports functioned as a gateway for youth to feel valued and to increase their sense of self-worth.

To make A Ganar possible, Fabian and the IDB team partnered with foundations and private companies, ensuring funding and employment opportunities for participants after graduation from the program. Partners included PepsiCo, Microsoft, the Nike Foundation, and the Carlos Slim Foundation. It was initially piloted in three countries—Brazil, Ecuador, and Uruguay—with local nonprofits running the day-to-day operations. Throughout the pilot phase, Fabian made it a priority to spend time with the local coaches and trainers. Fabian's job was to listen and do everything he could to ensure these leaders had the resources they needed. The program was successful, and soon expanded to nine additional countries in Latin America and the Caribbean, reaching more than 12,000 youth. To date, the IDB's sports-for-development initiatives have reached more than 89,000 people across 18 countries.

Fabian's work helped mainstream youth development into the IDB's operations. Today, it is common for large IDB projects to include components focused on supporting young people. That is perhaps the most lasting impact of Fabian's work at the institution. But after more than two decades at the IDB, it was time to move on.

"You have to listen to yourself. What you do has to be in harmony with your internal world," says Fabian. "That's how you ensure you are giving 100 percent of yourself."

Together with Mario Cader-Frech, his former MTV ally, Fabian recently launched KC Social Impact Lab, a consulting group that advises private and public organizations on development and outreach programs. They also partnered with Giulia D'Amico, the former CEO of One Laptop Per Child, which provides computers and educational programs for kids in the developing world. The three partners have extensive experience working with young people, and are all driven by a shared commitment to listening to and empowering others.

Fabian has built long-lasting professional relationships across the globe—from people in multilateral development banks, governments, and foundations, to investors and business executives, to academics and social entrepreneurs. Over the years, thanks to Fabian, I have met many of these people. They would often say something along the lines of, "Fabian is a good guy, he knows everybody and is always willing to make introductions and help you succeed, without taking credit for his help."

Fabian remembers that early in his career, this perception of his "good guy" status made him feel insecure. He was afraid that others thought he was naïve. Today, Fabian is more confident. He acknowledges that some people might say that "he is a good guy," thinking that he is naïve. But he believes it is more important to be in harmony with his inner convictions. He values connecting with others with generosity. It shows who he is as a person. And it is a big part of why others trust him.

Fabian's case is an example of the dynamic relationship between the inner and outer circles. By connecting with young people across the world, Fabian also connected with his inner circle. He learned to value his capacity to listen, to be a bridge, and create opportunities to lift up young people—opportunities just like the one he had been given.

KEY TAKEAWAYS

○ Listening and seeking to understand others helps you build meaningful relationships. Fabian did not assume what young leaders needed. He spent time with them, he was curious about their work and challenges, asked them what they needed, and exchanged ideas.

o By nourishing your outer circle, you also grow your inner circle—the two are connected in a dialectic dynamic. When Fabian met the IDB president, he did not know what he wanted to do in his career. Fabian was not sure what his calling was or what value he could bring to an organization. However, by engaging with others with an open mind, listening, and trying to help them, Fabian also connected with his inner circle. In turn, nurturing his inner circle helped Fabian gain confidence, keep growing, and be even more effective in supporting others.

FOSTERING TRUST
THE CASE OF AVI AND FRANK

Avi Hofman and Frank Taverner never imagined they would end up codirecting a major division at the International Finance Corporation (IFC), the private sector investment arm of the World Bank Group. They had heard of each other, shared a few meetings over the years, but did not really know each other. They had different management styles and were at different stages in their careers.

An American, Avi is soft-spoken, thoughtful and caring, but often comes across as serious, especially to those who don't know him. He practices yoga, meditates, and sometimes attends silent retreats—seeking internal harmony to be able to better listen to and connect with others. Avi had served as the director of various divisions, large and small, for more than 20 years, and had been responsible for setting up many of IFC's financial and risk management platforms. He knew the ins and outs of the organization, had become a trusted advisor on financial risk issues for CEOs over the years, and was now nearing retirement.

In contrast, Frank was just beginning to make his mark in the organization, with only a few management roles under his belt. Frustrated by the bureaucratic slowness of a large organization, he was eager to innovate and find ways for IFC to be more proactive and agile. A native of Zimbabwe, Frank is outgoing, likes to joke and mingle with staff, and pays little attention to organizational divisions and hierarchies.

So they were both surprised when the CEO asked them to codirect IFC's new corporate risk management division—which did not yet exist as such. It would be a merger of about 150 staff from more than five different departments with diverse organizational cultures. Avi and Frank were tasked with bringing this large and disjointed group together as one team to effectively identify financial risks and opportunities for IFC's operations, and advise senior leadership on how to address them. But first the two needed to build an "inner conversation" about their leadership goals so they could work well together.

Co-leadership for departments was a new management concept in IFC. The CEO was introducing it to increase collaboration among staff. With fewer, larger departments, he believed it would be easier for people to work with others. He also wanted more than one director to manage each department, so they could complement each other's strengths and staff could receive adequate attention. But co-leadership required a major cultural change. There was a risk that co-directors would end up competing instead of collaborating. At the same time, this new leadership model was being introduced amid a broader reorganization that was already creating a lot of uncertainty.

"There was a lot of dissatisfaction among staff," Avi told me. "If Frank and I were not going to get along well with each other, nobody would follow us."

Frank and Avi started meeting for early breakfasts. During these morning conversations they realized they both had strong technical backgrounds and, regardless of their different styles, cared deeply about their staff and work. They also understood that they could complement each other. Avi knew that times were changing and admired Frank's initiative to try out new ideas. It would be a great opportunity to innovate before his retirement. For his part, Frank respected Avi's expertise leading large teams through difficult times and fast-changing environments. His experience would be invaluable given the complexity of the challenge they were facing. As trust between them grew, they became the best ambassadors for each other—and for their staff.

Early on, Avi and Frank brought me to their team and over time I had the chance to get to know each of them. I once asked Avi, an observant Jew, what he had learned from Judaism that informed his leadership style, and he told me: "That you need to treat everybody fairly, no matter who they are." I also asked Frank what kind of leader he aspired to be and he said: "A genuine leader who cares about people. You have to walk the corridors, spend time with your team, learn about what they do, show them that you value their work as well as who they are as people."

From early conversations with staff, they knew people were anxious about the organizational changes. People did not know what their roles would be in the new structure, who they would report to, and, ultimately, whether their jobs were in jeopardy. Cognizant of this, one of their first acts as co-directors was to present the new department's organizational chart so that staff could see how the department would be structured and where they would fit. Avi and Frank wanted to send a clear message that they understood staff members' concerns and were there to support them.

They also made clear that the separate units in the organizational chart were just starting points. They wanted to create one team, not a group of units that operated in silos. They wanted people to collaborate with colleagues, focusing on what the department as a whole had to deliver for the rest of the organization: timely, high-quality risk analyses delivered in a way that made it easy for senior management to make decisions.

Some might argue that the two leaders were too quick in deciding the new structure and should have taken more time to consult with all the people involved. Instead they prioritized not adding to staff uncertainty. They had a clear idea of how they wanted to organize the department—agreed upon during their many breakfasts—and wanted to be transparent about their plan with the team. Frank and Avi made clear that they would make modifications along the way as needed but that the team should not expect major changes. They wanted people to feel safe and empowered to get to work.

A few months in, their efforts began to pay off. While other IFC co-directors were embroiled in turf wars with their departments going through endless changes, Avi and Frank's team had already begun to deliver. "We showed [senior leadership] the organizational chart and work program, and they were happy we were bringing a solution and a clear idea of what we would do, instead of asking them what to do. That's what Avi and I did, and it worked well ... they just told us, 'let us know if you need something from us,'" Frank reflected.

For Avi and Frank, fostering trust was paramount. In addition to being transparent about major staffing decisions, they worked diligently to get to know each staff member, understand everyone's unique contributions, and encourage a spirit of continuous improvement. For example, they created a series of coffees with the directors, inviting small groups of staff—usually at the same level but from different units—to come and share what was on their minds. Frank and Avi would follow up with individual thank-you notes, mentioning something that person had contributed during the gathering and that they especially valued.

Avi and Frank also did their best to implement ideas suggested by staff. For instance, some administrative staff shared their frustration that they were underutilized, and suggested areas in which they could contribute such as basic research or event planning. Frank and Avi discussed the issue with managers and brainstormed with them about ways to broaden responsibilities and skill-sets. Over time, some administrative staff began to assist on research assignments. This made their work days more interesting and increased their value to their teams. Avi and Frank also adopted ideas from more senior staff such as how to better manage the organization's financial reserves or deal with unexpected turmoil in the international credit markets.

To ensure the department worked together as one team, they introduced several projects that required collaboration from people in different units. For example, every quarter, the department presented a comprehensive assessment of the financial risks the organization was facing. Staff from all levels were encouraged to participate in brainstorming and planning sessions. People got the opportunity to voice their ideas and get exposure with the directors. When the directors presented this quarterly report to senior management, they would often bring staff with them who had contributed, no matter their seniority.

Frank and Avi were also keen on clear communication. They understood that the department worked on very important, but highly technical, issues and that few people in the organization had the background or the time to fully grasp their analyses. From the beginning, I spent a lot of time helping Avi and Frank develop clear messaging. But they believed that effective communication should be a priority for the entire department, not just for them as directors. Therefore, they also asked me to put together a plan to train managers and key technical specialists across the department, so they could all become more effective communicators. We organized a series of workshops and I provided communication coaching on an ongoing basis. People learned how to use storytelling to share their ideas and develop clear, appealing presentations. The department gained a reputation for effective communication and soon other parts of the organization began to adopt its approach. (In the appendix, you can find a short article, based on my experience working with Frank and Avi, with tips on how to develop and deliver an effective presentation.)

Avi and Frank's case is a good example of two leaders who managed to build trust with each other, and then extend that trust to their staff. In a time of organizational uncertainty, Avi and Frank transformed several heterogeneous groups into one cohesive team and delivered a critical function for the rest of the organization.

KEY TAKEAWAYS

○ Building trust with others is essential to growing your outer circle. Avi and Frank spent significant time getting to know each other and finding a way to complement each other's styles to best support staff. That process helped them build trust between them.

○ Listening to and empowering others will help you create a high-performing team. Frank and Avi listened to their staff and showed them with concrete actions that they cared about them. In a context of organizational uncertainty, they lowered anxiety by sharing the organizational structure early, creating space for staff to be heard, and launching projects in which team members could be proactive, suggesting and implementing new ideas. They took staff input seriously and made them feel valued by providing recognition.

○ Understanding your audience's needs and priorities is crucial to communicating effectively. Avi and Frank understood that senior management needed clear messaging that could be grasped quickly and used for their decision-making. Not only did they spend time improving their own communications, but they also invested resources so their staff members could become better communicators.

DEVELOPING A SHARED NARRATIVE

A key part of expanding your outer circle is leveraging a well-crafted shared narrative. A powerful narrative can propel a company, a social cause, or even just a small team toward productive, energetic cooperation and collaboration. You want to create a narrative that resonates with your audience and inspires a shared sense of purpose and direction. As with personal narratives, shared—or "collective"—narratives consist of three parts: what, how, and why.

○ **What.** For example, you could say: "We are a newspaper that publishes breaking news," or "We are an investment firm supporting businesses in developing countries."

○ **How.** For instance, you could say: "We use online ads to finance our operations, so everybody can access our content for free," or "We have people based in each of the countries where we work, which allows us to be close to clients and understand local markets."

○ **Why.** For example, you could say: "We believe that an informed public is essential to an open, inclusive, and free society," or

"We believe in supporting businesses that create jobs where they are needed the most and bring dignity to people."

The what and the how are important pieces of information, but are not enough to create an appealing narrative that connects with others and inspires them to take action (e.g., proactively contribute ideas to the team or own and execute an important organizational initiative). To do that, you'll need a powerful why. Take Google. The what is easy—it's the suite of products that the company offers: search, maps, Gmail, etc. The how is the way leadership approaches their work: hiring the best talent, fostering innovation within the company, and focusing on the end user. But it's the why that makes the difference. Google's mission is to "organize the world's information and make it universally accessible and useful." In its very early days, this mission created an ethos that bonded the company with its employees and users, driving every product release, every acquisition, every hire. And without it, Google would not have become the technology giant it is today.

You don't need to be the CEO of a global company to shape a collective narrative. Smaller initiatives can also benefit. Imagine you work for a company that is going through a reorganization and you are asked to head a new division that merges five different functions: accounting, human resources, policies and procedures, knowledge management, and training. Employees are upset; they feel senior management does not understand the importance of these functions and is bundling them together in a way that does not make sense.

Instead of mollifying staff with false promises of continuity, you could ask them to work with you to develop a collective narrative that brings together these different functions. In focus groups and interviews, you discover that staff across the five areas care about delivering the best possible support to the rest of the organization, and they would like to see themselves as the backbone that allows employees and management to deliver on the company's mission. There's your why. Armed with that powerful narrative, employees start to imagine more and better ways to put internal clients front and center and provide integrated services for problems that span multiple support functions. Now, the new division provides even more value for the organization.

A collective narrative of this style can help staff come together as one team, find meaning in the work they do, and increase the value they deliver. In the next section, you will hear about Alzbeta, who fostered a collective narrative which did exactly that. The shared narrative also helped transform a function that was perceived as marginal into a mainstream operational area key for the organization's success.

As with a personal narrative, you can craft a collective narrative by weaving together specific stories. The basic elements for collective stories are similar to the ones we described for personal stories: challenge, choice, outcome, and learning. The difference is that here you will be talking about a collective, about "us," not just "you."

Typically, stories that make up a personal narrative are drawn from past experiences. You already faced the challenge, made a choice, and know the outcome. When you create a collective narrative, you want to talk about past shared experiences to develop a sense of common history. But you also want to talk about a challenge the collective has not yet addressed. In that sense, the desired outcome and the learning are a vision you will be offering for the future.

You may also want to include a call to action. This is an invitation to others to be part of the solution to a common challenge. This should be as specific as possible. It is not enough to tell people to "support this initiative". Rather, think about what you want the other person to do after hearing your story. Tell them what concrete actions they can take to support it: work for this team, talk to clients about it, or prepare a proposal on how to manage this or that component.

Below are some questions to think about collective stories:

O **Challenge.** Why is this challenge relevant for all of you? What would happen if you do not address it?

O **Choice.** What are the options you all face? Which one should you choose and why? What actions would you have to take to follow through?

O **Outcome.** What would happen if you take the desired option? If not? What is the vision you are asking people to pursue?

O **Learning.** What are the shared values at play in the story? What's the main message you want others to take away?

O **Call to action.** Leave your audience with a clear ask. What can they do to be part of the solution?

Ideally, you want to connect your personal narrative to the collective one. By sharing a personal challenge that aligns with the collective challenge, you will be showing you personally relate to and care about others' experiences. Imagine a mid-level manager who has lost several talented young employees because they don't feel the company cares about their career growth. She believes a company mentoring program might help. She knows that to get support from senior management, she'll need to show that other managers are on board. She reaches out to her peers and shares her challenge trying to retain young staff, suggesting that it may be a common issue across the organization. This is a narrative that resonates with her peers and they decide to join the program.

In cases where neat alignment between personal and collective narratives is not possible, there should at least be coherence, not dissonance. Let's say someone is appointed to lead an environmental project—heading a team of committed and seasoned environmental professionals—but has a long history of working for Big Oil. To gain his team's support, he'll need to find a way to articulate a narrative that explains why he went from working for Big Oil to leading an environmental initiative. (Perhaps he regrets being part of these companies and wants to redeem himself). The key is to be genuine with others. If not, you will never gain people's trust.

Let's imagine another person who has been asked to lead an environmental project but has no experience in the field. However, she has never been employed by corporations that damage the environment. She has shown she cares about the public good by volunteering at a homeless shelter. And she has valuable management skills that will help the team increase its efficiency and delivery. That person might not be the "natural" leader for an environmental project but can be perceived as genuine and win over her new team and other key stakeholders.

Ultimately, you want to show others that you truly care about the collective success. You want them to see that you have their best interest in mind. If they believe in you, you will be well positioned to mold a shared narrative that provides purpose and strategic direction. Next, we'll learn about Alzbeta Klein, a powerhouse at the World Bank Group, who managed to completely transform one of the organization's operational functions by rallying her staff around a collective narrative that they crafted together.

BE THE FLOW
THE CASE OF ALZBETA

Originally from Czechoslovakia, Alzbeta Klein fled the Communist Bloc in the turbulent summer of 1989 when she had just turned 23. Alone, a refugee, Alzbeta made it to Canada. There, she worked full time while completing her education as an engineer and economist. After being selected for a coveted spot in the World Bank Group Young Professionals Program, she moved to Washington, DC to work for the International Finance Corporation (IFC), the part of the Group that supports the private sector.

"You have to take ownership of your own life; you can't depend on anybody else," she told me.

She quickly became a rising star, structuring complex investment deals that delivered solid financial returns while spreading social benefits to local communities. And unlike many other investment officers, Alzbeta made a point of staying in touch with the local partners to make sure the investment performed over time. "Structuring a new investment may take seven or eight months," she explained. "But managing the investment and making sure it performs may take seven or eight years."

Alzbeta believes strongly that the portfolio management function—the management of existing investments—is essential to building a sustainable business. Problems arise, she tells people, when the spotlight is just on bringing new business, and managing the existing portfolio becomes a second-tier function.

After years at IFC and a series of challenging positions—such as representing the organization in Russia and being chief of staff for the CEO—a promotion positioned Alzbeta as the director of a major division overseeing non-financial risks. She was ready to make her mark at IFC.

It wouldn't be easy. The division had, over time, lost a clear sense of direction and relevance within the broader organization. According to the most recent staff satisfaction survey, just 10 percent of department staff were satisfied with their jobs. And only six months into the job, things got hairier. Senior leadership launched a major restructuring and asked her to take another division under her wing: portfolio management.

But just like so many investment officers, some members of senior leadership did not see portfolio management as a priority, which had greatly demoralized the staff. To turn the situation around, Alzbeta needed to build on her track record and reputation, and establish a productive outer conversation with her immediate team, IFC's network of portfolio specialists, new business people, and senior management. It was time to redefine how business would be run at IFC.

Alzbeta took about 100 days to understand what was working and what needed to be fixed. She talked to everyone on her team as well as people in other divisions who interacted with the portfolio function. "I had six or seven meetings a day," she recalled. Alzbeta also spent time with these people in more casual settings, such as lunches, where people often feel more relaxed. She has a special gift for connecting with people and knows how to create the environment for others to feel comfortable with her and open up.

Once Alzbeta had a deeper grasp of what needed to be done, she began to foster a new narrative about portfolio management. That collective narrative came to define and re-energize hundreds of employees across the institution. Her efforts were directed toward three groups: portfolio specialists, portfolio assistants, and the central portfolio team.

PORTFOLIO SPECIALISTS

A loosely-connected group of staff scattered across various investment divisions, portfolio specialists (portfolio managers in IFC speak) felt unheard by management and business development colleagues. As a consequence, morale had plummeted. Dispersed across different offices all over the world, they had few opportunities to interact with each other face-to-face and develop personal relationships.

Alzbeta knew they needed to go from a group of people who shared a title to a team that shared knowledge and supported each other. If portfolio specialists could bring the collective expertise of the network to each of their engagements with internal clients, in each of their respective divisions, their standing in the organization would rise.

Alzbeta organized a series of in-person workshops for these staff to connect and share ideas. "I remember the first workshop we conducted in Istanbul, people realized how much we could achieve together," Alzbeta told me. There, the network developed a document, ratified by all participants, that stated who they wanted to be as a network, how they wanted to work together, and what they aimed to contribute to the broader organization and clients. The agreement ended with the phrase by Elif Shafak: "Do not go with the flow. Be the flow."

Through the creation of the "Istanbul Agreement," the portfolio specialists took ownership of their new narrative. "Portfolio matters" became their motto. And after a few more workshops and smaller group interactions, the network began to coalesce. It was now time to show the rest of the organization what they did and why it mattered.

They started with natural allies, inviting colleagues and senior executives who understood the importance of portfolio management to the workshop series. As they began to appreciate the innovative work that the portfolio network was doing, they became ambassadors to the rest of the organization.

After many months of hard work, the network invited the CEO to its next workshop. I remember being there; you could feel in the air that something special was about to happen. The CEO was glad to see how the specialists had taken ownership of the challenge to reshape the portfolio function (instead of waiting for senior leadership to tell them what to do). Before leaving, he made a promise of full support, so they could continue to spread the change throughout IFC.

PORTFOLIO ASSISTANTS

If Alzbeta had not taken the time to engage with people at all levels, she may have missed a key piece of the reorganization's success: portfolio assistance. Portfolio assistants were junior professionals who provided support to portfolio specialists, managing portfolio databases and preparing reports. Portfolio assistants were uniquely positioned to influence up more senior staff who needed their support—just as long as they provided high-quality service.

As she had done with the portfolio specialists, Alzbeta created a network of portfolio assistants, so that they could exchange knowledge and support each other. Alzbeta's team organized a series of team-building workshops and virtual meetings, an online portal, and a robust training curriculum. These efforts empowered the assistants to serve their internal clients with industry best practices.

CENTRAL PORTFOLIO TEAM

Alzbeta's immediate team was responsible for conducting data gathering and reporting activities to support the portfolio specialists, as well as provide senior management with consolidated information on the company's portfolio performance. Alzbeta needed to achieve several things with this team, but ultimately, she needed this group to go from a reporting division to a business partner for the organization.

The team had lost touch with their internal clients' needs and were doing their jobs mechanically. They weren't stopping to think about what they needed to achieve and what was the best way of getting there. Alzbeta wanted them to see that she would be their best champion, but that they needed to be open to change and focus on what mattered to their clients.

"I want open-minded people that can bring different perspectives," she explained. "I want people who focus on what matters for clients and collaborate across the division, beyond formal hierarchies, to add value." For some, this new approach rubbed the wrong way. Some people left. To replace them, Alzbeta hired people that not only had the right technical skills, but also were a good fit for the more dynamic and horizontal structure she was creating.

Alzbeta knows that sometimes she can come across as tough. For the most part though, people who care about making a difference at their jobs see the bright side of Alzbeta's toughness. She uses it to clear the space for her team to do its best work. "When people get to know Alzbeta and see her actions, how she goes out of her way to support her team and tries to create opportunities for people, they realize how much she cares about them," a colleague who has known her for years told me.

The people that were able to leave their comfort zones and adapt to the changes soon saw their productivity increase. They began enjoying their day-to-day work and saw their contributions being recognized. People felt excited to be part of special initiatives that were relevant for the success of the company, and saw opportunities to get exposure and show their potential.

After three years, Alzbeta was promoted to another role. By then, senior leadership and most investment staff understood the importance of portfolio management. A cultural change was underway—the organization had modified some operational processes for new business professionals to have clear responsibility on projects from end-to-end and for portfolio specialists to be part of every new investment. Alzbeta's approach to managing investments was now a key part of the institution's way of managing its business. She had aligned her inner circle with her outer circle—and expanded its influence.

In complex change processes we can think of the broader outer conversation—the outer circle—as multiple conversations that interconnect and reinforce each other. When they begin to align is when the outer circle expands and produces a change or impact. As people started to connect and cooperate the circle began to expand and influence the rest of the organization.

This is what Alzbeta did. She constructed a shared narrative about why portfolio was crucial for the organization. That narrative gave the portfolio network, her immediate team, as well as other stakeholders a sense of shared purpose. Alzbeta knew why portfolio management was crucial and what that narrative would look like, and she shared that vision with others. But it was her emphasis on others taking ownership that was the key to her success.

KEY TAKEAWAYS

○ Fostering a collective narrative helps you bring people together, inspiring a sense of shared purpose and setting a common direction. Alzbeta worked with the portfolio staff to craft a shared narrative that instilled a sense of collective purpose and helped transform a function that was perceived as marginal into a mainstream operational area.

○ Aligning your personal narrative to the collective one shows others that you truly care about the collective success and have their best interest in mind. Alzbeta brought to the portfolio function her reputation as an investment professional who cared about portfolio management.

○ People want to be heard. From the beginning, Alzbeta had an idea of what was needed, but she also created the space for others to feel empowered, take ownership, and shape the narrative and the future of the portfolio management function.

CONNECTING ACROSS CULTURES

I often encounter talented professionals, who have all the traits and skills to lead effectively, who tell me that working with people from a different culture, and frequently in a foreign language, is a key obstacle to their success. I get it. I have spent most of my professional career outside my native country of Argentina, and I support both Spanish- and English-speaking leaders as a communications specialist. But in our globalizing world, professionals need to be ready to communicate with people whose native language and culture is different from their own.

Even professionals who have achieved a substantial level of fluency in the relevant foreign language may still lack confidence in their ability to be understood or to be taken seriously. What's more, this challenge goes beyond language. I have met many seasoned professionals working with people from a different culture but who speak the same language, feeling this same kind of insecurity. They're afraid of accidentally offending someone, misinterpreting or misusing colloquial terms and phrases, or sounding out of touch. They constantly doubt themselves. Due to that lack of confidence, they are hesitant to hone their skills or ask for help, and their ability to communicate suffers.

Connecting with people across cultural and language divides takes practice. As you practice, you'll likely make mistakes. Most people will laugh it off—or gently correct you—especially if they believe you're making an honest, respectful effort. Here is what I have found to help—from my own personal experiences, as well as what I have seen work for many of my clients.

LISTEN FIRST

Making sense of your audience's values, desires, goals, opinions, prejudices, etc. is never an easy task, and when cultural differences or language barriers are in the mix, it becomes even more difficult. To succeed, you need to start listening. Really listening.

We can think of three basic levels of listening, based on where you put your attention as you engage with the other person:

1. **Self-listening.** We all have a tendency to be here, as most of the time our focus is on ourselves. But this is not actual listening. It is more like having a sense of what the other person is saying while waiting for our turn to talk. If you find yourself thinking about what you will say next while the other person is talking, you are probably at this level.

2. **Intent-listening.** Here you are intensely focused on what the other person is saying. You are not distracted by your own thoughts about the past or the future. Your own ideas don't get in the way of you hearing the other person. In this level, you start connecting with the other person.

3. **Deep-listening.** This is the level that helps us truly connect with others. You are not only paying attention to what others say, but also what they mean—what they do not say, how they express their emotions, what their body language tells you. It's about giving the other person your full cognitive and emotional

attention in a non-judgmental way and seeing what happens. Deep-listening does not mean you have to be silent. Be curious, ask questions. Open your mind and learn as much as possible about the other person.

Moving from self-listening toward deep-listening requires practice. It is hard work, often exhausting. But it pays off. As you increase your capacity to focus on the other person, you will have a fuller understanding of what he or she actually means. Over time, you may find that this increased level of attention allows you to see things others do not. When people interact with others in a familiar context, they often do it mechanically and may miss what the other person is actually trying to communicate. When you are in a "foreign" environment, you bring a different perspective, see things through a different lens, and appreciate what others do not even register. Others may come to value this and seek out your perspective more and more.

CLARIFY YOUR INNER CONVERSATION

As we discussed in the Inner Circle section, it is important to have clarity on what your goals are, why you want to engage with others, and what you want to achieve. Clarity of communication follows clarity of thought.

BUILD UP YOUR PERSONAL COMMUNICATION TEAM

Journalists have editors. Politicians have speech writers. You are being asked to communicate with people who do not share your background, and perhaps to do so in a second or third language. Why not ask for some help?

If you are in a formal leadership position and have the budget, you could hire a communications advisor. But if not, you can do it in other ways. Share your writing with a native speaker who you know is a good communicator. Ask someone who understands the local culture to help you rehearse your presentation. Truly, there is nothing wrong with enlisting a little bit of help. Actually, there is a lot right about it. Your communication will be clear; you won't be asking your audience to decipher your messages for you. They will appreciate it.

For example, one of my previous supervisors had a role that required extensive traveling to meet with clients. Even though most clients spoke English (as did she), before visiting a country for the first time, she would seek out staff from that place working at the global headquarters in Washington, DC. She would ask about both the local culture and the business environment. Once in the country, she would do the same with local staff before meeting with clients. This practice helped her gain an initial understanding of the clients' backgrounds.

I'll talk more about building up your team of advisors later in the book, but for now, remember that you'll need to establish a two-way relationship with these helpers and guides. Figure out what you can do for them—and be sure to acknowledge their assistance whenever possible. Just be careful not to expect or ask for too much. At the end of the day, you need to rely on yourself—your thoughts, your words, your narrative—to connect with those around you in a genuine manner—whether they grew up down the street or half a world away.

Generally speaking, the ideas described here on how to engage and communicate across cultures are not that different from those to connect with people from your own culture. Ultimately, genuine communication is about having clarity about what you want to share and taking the time to understand the other person, so you can connect in an open and sincere way. However, when engaging across cultures, you may not be familiar with the way others see things and express themselves. You have to be even more aware of the importance of listening, being curious, and asking questions. Effective leadership communication across cultures and languages is possible, but it requires time and effort. Next, we'll get to know David Auerbach, a social entrepreneur who jumped feet first into the challenges—and opportunities—of cross-cultural connection and communication.

A ONE-WAY TICKET
THE CASE OF DAVID

Davd Auerbach had scarcely been in Kenya a week before he met David Kitusa, a local who ran the country's branch of Kiva, an international nonprofit that promotes access to financing in underserved communities. David told Kitusa about the company he was planning to set up with two business school classmates that would bring sanitation services to some of the poorest areas of the country.

The idea, David explained, was to build and install toilets that did not rely on an existing sewer system—making them perfect for slums and other areas with extreme poverty and little or no infrastructure. The company would then collect the waste, convert it into organic fertilizer, and sell it to farmers. Kitusa found David's idea intriguing, but assumed he was just another Western "kid" spending some adventurous months, perhaps a year, in Kenya to bulk up his resume. So when Kitusa asked him how long he was planning on staying in Kenya, the answer caught him completely off guard. "I just got a one-way ticket," David said simply.

Ten years later, David leads a thriving and innovative business, is married to a Kenyan woman, and has made enduring friendships in the country. His company, Sanergy, provides toilets for more than 150,000 people a day, a large portion of them in slums. In 2019 alone, they collected more than 12,000 tons of waste, which they treated and converted into valuable end-products such as organic fertilizer, helping local farmers increase harvests by 30 percent. Sanergy's success is the result of an innovative business idea and thorough implementation. David's genuine leadership style has been essential to that success. As we will see, David's calling to go to Kenya and develop this project was the product of his inner conversation, and his success hinged on getting the outer conversations right.

After spending most of his childhood in the United Kingdom, David returned to the United States for college. "I didn't know what I wanted to do in my life, so I thought an education that would give me flexibility to explore different things would be a good fit for me," David recalls. "A liberal arts school in the US is more flexible than in the UK where you have to choose your major before starting your studies, when you are not even 18."

He enrolled at Yale, attracted to the open-minded atmosphere and the sense of endless options to explore. David did his best to take advantage of the possibilities in front of him. He enrolled in diverse classes and met people from everywhere. "My mom called once to ask why I hadn't reached out to her in two weeks—she thought I might be sick. I was just enjoying this new world." In his senior year, he landed a foreign policy internship at the Center for American Progress, a progressive public policy think tank in Washington, DC. "That experience helped me forge my political identity and also make some long-lasting professional connections," David explains.

Right after college, he spent a year in China, teaching English and storytelling skills to a class of 200 pre-teens. He also counseled older students through the American university application process. When he wasn't teaching, David traveled across the country, meeting people who had started their own businesses. "It helped me understand the power of entrepreneurship in a country growing so fast but still with so much poverty and unmet needs,"

David says. During his travels, he saw firsthand how not having proper sanitation systems held back progress. It made people sick, and was a major obstacle for economic and social development. After China, David went to New York City to work for two global nonprofit organizations that support social entrepreneurship in developing countries: the Clinton Global Initiative and Endeavor. There David learned about fundraising, communication, and partnership building. But soon enough, he was back in school, pursuing an MBA at the MIT Sloan School of Management, a school known for its focus on entrepreneurship.

For one school assignment, David and two classmates, Lindsay Stradley and Ani Vallabhaneni, were asked to develop a business plan to help address widespread poverty. The plan had to tackle a poverty challenge faced by one billion people or more around the globe. Drawing on their experiences working in developing countries and in growing cities, they designed a plan to provide sanitation services in urban slums. The idea for Sanergy was born.

While most of David's MIT classmates spent their last semester trying to secure a job at a top-tier company, he and his partners spent their time traveling the US seeking potential investors for Sanergy. For the young co-founders, this would be one of their greatest challenges. With no experience running a business, no formal education in sanitation, and no ties to Kenya, the three had to find a way to convince investors that their money would be used wisely. They needed to create trust, get investors to believe in the company's social impact mission, and convince them of its potential to deliver profits and become financially sustainable. They had to show they knew what they were doing.

By crafting a thorough business plan and being upfront about what they didn't know, David and his co-founders were able to build trust with investors. They promised to surround themselves with the right people to close their knowledge gaps. They explained they would hire sanitation experts and local staff with a good understanding of the slums and other places where Sanergy would work. The fact that they were willing to move to Kenya and stay there for the long-term helped assuage investors' concerns.

They managed to secure funding for the first six months—just enough to start setting up the company, which included making legal arrangements, hiring the first employees, and building and installing the initial toilets. This all gave them something to show for future fundraising efforts.

But if David and his co-founders wanted to stand a chance at succeeding in a foreign environment, they needed to develop a thorough, culturally-aware business strategy. So, they spent a month crisscrossing the country, engaging with locals about their vision for Sanergy and learning as much as they could about the local culture. They quickly learned that, even in the private sector, most Kenyans were accustomed to a rigid hierarchical culture. It would take time to create the horizontal and entrepreneurial environment they believed was crucial to attracting smart and proactive people—the kind of talent they wanted for Sanergy.

Their travels also underscored the importance of engaging with those who could get deep into the slums and gather real feedback from communities. They would need people who could, for example, find out whether women felt comfortable using the toilets, and what could be done to improve safety. These "insiders" would help David and his co-founders understand the unique challenges Sanergy might face. Ultimately, the co-founders decided to set up Sanergy offices right in the middle of one of the slums.[15] Today, nine out of every ten employees in the company are from Kenya, and six out of every ten live in the communities it serves.

Some years ago, when I visited Sanergy's operations, one of the employees told me:

"When you get to know David, you want to be part of his team. He has a real passion for the work he is doing; it's consistent with who he is as a person. When he talks about his previous professional experiences, in China or in the US, you see how he used each of those experiences to learn and become the leader he is today ... and you feel that he cares about us who are just starting our professional journeys. He wants to create a supporting environment, so we can learn and discover the kind of professionals we want to become."

As its reputation grew, Sanergy started to attract more and more Kenyans who had left the country for better educational opportunities, but had since returned, eager to make a difference in their home country. Creating space for these Kenyans helped David and his partners continue to bridge the gap between their "outsider" status and the local culture. These young Kenyans have also become valuable communications advisors.

In the office, David and his partners try to create an open, horizontal corporate culture—they don't even have assigned desks or offices. "Once, I got to the office and found an intern in my 'usual' seat," David told me with a smile. The intern can hardly be blamed—David is rarely at "his" desk. He walks everywhere, meeting his staff where they are instead of expecting them to come to him. David often shares relaxed lunches with his teams at the office. People are not afraid to share ideas or ask about the company's performance and future plans.

David regularly visits the facility where Sanergy builds the toilets and the plant where they convert waste into organic fertilizer. He also spends time with the "field teams," such as business development or maintenance staff, who are the closest to the population Sanergy serves. He listens to their concerns and pays attention to their ideas. Here's an example in David's words:

"In our initial model, toilets were run by entrepreneurs [such as somebody who owns a small shop in the slum], who would situate the toilets in areas with high-foot traffic. We got great usage, and so thought that the model was working well. But then we started to hear from our sales team in the community that residents really wanted toilets within their residential compounds, ensuring that they have 24/7, private experiences. To do this, we needed to work with landlords, who control the compounds. So instead of paying for the asset upfront, which landlords did not want to do, we began charging on an ongoing leasing basis. Sales increased by three times and we are serving our customers in a much better way."

Today, the company has a staff of more than 250 employees. David would love for his sanitation model to scale up to new places. But he also understands that his company's success has a lot to do with him and his partners taking the time to truly connect with a large network of local people, inside and outside the company. He knows that there is no shortcut for genuine human connection.

KEY TAKEAWAYS

○ Aligning your inner and outer circles provides you with motivation and purpose. David's desire to build a business with social impact in Kenya drew on a deep exploration of his inner values and goals. That gave him the determination and perseverance needed to embed himself in a foreign culture and grow a successful business.

○ Honesty fosters trust. David and his partners lacked experience and subject matter expertise, but they were upfront with investors about what they did not know. That openness, together with thorough planning and solid principles, convinced investors that they could trust the young entrepreneurs.

○ Deep listening is crucial to help you understand another culture. Before starting up their business, the three founders spent a month crisscrossing the country, learning as much as they could about the local culture.

○ Building your team of "communications advisors" helps you connect to people from a different culture. The majority of Sanergy employees are from Kenya, helping David and his partners bridge the cultural gap.

BUILDING YOUR NETWORK OF TRUSTED ADVISORS

Behind every great leader is a circle of trusted mentors, allies, and close colleagues. No one can do it alone. But that kind of network doesn't happen by accident. Leaders start building relationships and partnerships early— maintaining, as well as growing, this critical network over time.

As you plan your own networking strategy, use the Expanding Circle as a framework. Start with the inner conversation to explore your values and ambitions and define your goals for approaching others. The goals can be generic ("building social capital for my career") or specific ("landing a new job"). In fact, it's best to build your network when you have generic goals—when you are not asking for anything—and then use it when you have specific goals—when you'll likely be asking others to do something for you.

Then, move into the outer circle, identifying who you need to approach. You might not know the specific *who* yet, but you can

identify certain characteristics of people you'd like to connect with—
say, someone with experience in a specific field or a former professor
or boss who has a good grasp of your strengths and weaknesses.
You can think of networking as a tree. You will contact someone,
and that person might not be exactly who you are looking for,
but they might know other people you should connect with. That
branch of the tree will sprout another one or more, and so on and
so on. Just be sure to keep nurturing the original relationships.
You never know when you might need them. Later, we'll hear
about Rayco Bejarano García, a young international relations
professional who has created an impressive networking tree,
and approaches each connection with curiosity—not an agenda.

Now, let's think about the different people you want in your
network. It is important to cultivate various kinds of relationships.
It will vary depending on your field, career level, and goals, but
we can boil these relationships down to six categories: mentor,
promoter, connector, role model, peer, and mentee.

Mentor. This is someone with relevant experience who you
trust and who you believe has your best interests in mind. A
mentor invests in you because he cares about you and believes
in you. He does not expect anything in return. Ideally, a mentor
understands your career challenges, is a good listener, and knows
how to ask the right questions to help you find your own answers.
With the right amount of wisdom, he can help you develop your
own unique style and journey, rather than replicating someone
else's path.

You can have more than one mentor—at the same phase in
your career or at different moments throughout it. Mentors need
not work in your specific field; many of the challenges you will
face in your career go beyond your technical area of expertise
(say, negotiating a salary or dealing with difficult bosses). In fact,
having a perspective from someone outside your field can be
refreshing and eye-opening.

You can also find a helpful perspective from a mentor who is in your field but works for a different organization. This person might have a good grasp of the kind of work you do and will be able to help you think through tricky situations without a hidden agenda. However, each mentorship relationship is unique, and you can find a good mentor within your organization. Indeed, a supervisor can become a great mentor. Just ensure that your mentor has your best interests in mind and encourages you to grow and think critically about your career development.

Try to keep mentoring relationships alive for the long run. These are the people you can turn to throughout your career—they'll be there for you when you need them. And think about ways you can give back to them. You probably won't be giving them career advice, but a genuine "thank you" or show of appreciation can go a long way.

Promoter. This is someone who can help you land a job, get a promotion, or succeed in a project you are running. They might also be mentors—but not always. In some cases, a promoter will help you because she is expecting something in return or it is in her best interest—say, she wants the person who gets the open position to be someone she can trust. A promoter might help you today, but you cannot be sure that she will be there for you in the future. More than once, I have confused a promoter with a mentor and ended up disappointed. Don't make the same mistake.

Connector. This is someone willing to introduce you to others. Getting a phone number or email address is easy. An introduction by someone who has credibility and a good reputation with the person you would like to meet is not. This kind of introduction is like an endorsement. Of course, once the connection is made, it will be up to you to live up to that endorsement.

Connectors can be mentors, promoters, or simply people who know people you would like to meet. Connectors are not necessarily the ones who go around a cocktail party greeting everyone or have thousands of LinkedIn connections. It is not about the quantity but the quality of their relationships. When you approach a connector, be ready with a compelling personal story and a clear ask. This will help them understand who you are, what you are looking for, and how they can help you. You should also be open to their unique insights and expertise. You'll learn more, and forge a stronger relationship if you show genuine interest in them—not just the people they know!

Role model. This is someone whose career you admire, whether or not they are in your field. Ideally, you would like role models to become mentors (or connectors). However, if that's not possible, you can still learn a tremendous amount by understanding how they became the professionals they are. Don't be afraid to share your admiration. In fact, they will likely appreciate it and be inclined to share their experiences with you.

Peer. Many people spend most of their time trying to connect "up" and forget to establish meaningful relationships with coworkers or colleagues at a similar career level. I believe that's a mistake. You can learn as much from peers as from those on a higher rung of the career ladder. Your peers are closer to the issues you are facing now and can share meaningful lessons about how they've faced similar situations. Peers may even be teammates or colleagues you have to partner with. Strong, meaningful relationships will help you cooperate and get the best out of those partnerships.

Mentee. It is never too early to start mentoring others. Emerging professionals can offer a fresh perspective and rarely come to you with hidden agendas or office politics. They will tell you what they see and think. Mentoring someone can be a valuable learning experience for you as well. See it as an investment in your future. Today, someone is just starting in your field, but tomorrow that same person can be a potential client or employer. Taking on a mentee also allows you an important opportunity to be generous with your time and your knowledge. You may not always be able to give back to all of your networking relationships—but you can give forward.

Not all relationships you foster will fit neatly into one of these six categories—and you'll likely see these relationships change over time (a peer into a promoter or a role model into a mentor). But whether you are just starting to build your network or you are growing existing relationships, consider it a long-term investment. Talking to people for the first time can feel awkward. But engaging in those initial conversations is just the beginning. By nurturing these relationships over years—decades, even!—your connections become a source of enjoyment and continuous learning. If you value your network and show true appreciation, they will share with you their experiences and knowledge. They will help you and enrich your professional—and personal—life throughout the years. We'll hear more about this with the case of Sam Hendel, a sharp-witted finance professional who, against all odds, built a hugely disruptive technology company in the middle of the 2008 financial crisis. But first, let's turn to Rayco.

BEGINNING WITH CURIOSITY
THE CASE OF RAYCO

Rayco Bejarano García comes from a working-class family in Spain's Canary Islands—the first in his family to graduate from college. His father works as a security guard and his mother as an assistant teacher in a kindergarten. Although his parents always supported his love of learning, there was no family money or connections to help him along the way. When asked what has been the key to his professional development so far, he responds simply, "Curiosity. First, to look for scholarships to study in Spain and abroad, then to find internships, and finally to develop a network of connections. Yes, curiosity."

Now in his early thirties, Rayco became interested in media and communications as a young child. He remembers being at home while his mother cleaned the house—always listening to the same radio station. (Rayco would later intern at the same radio station early in his career.) After graduating with honors with a degree in journalism from the local university, Rayco jumped at the chance to go abroad to gain some professional experience and continue his studies. Curiosity—and tenacity—landed him an internship in Tanzania and scholarships to study in London and Madrid.

It wasn't an easy road. "I was able to study in Madrid thanks to a scholarship; I did not have any other money," Rayco recalls. "After the first semester I went back home, because it was cheaper than staying in Madrid during the school break. For some reason, there was a delay in the disbursement of the scholarship and I did not have any money to go back to Madrid. I was desperate. I wrote to the professors, asking them to please wait for me. The money finally arrived—late—but it arrived. Luckily, I only lost a week of classes."

After receiving his master's degree from the Universidad Autónoma de Madrid, Rayco returned to the Canary Islands to work for a local newspaper. "I really enjoyed it. The pay was not very much, but I think that working in journalism helped me channel my curiosity. You need to go out there, talk to people, and find out as much as you can about the news you are covering," Rayco explains.

But after his experiences outside the Islands, he wanted to further explore the world. So, he signed up for a free graduate program in international business. He was not sure he would learn much (he did) but he knew that the best students would be awarded a year-long internship at a multilateral development organization. Top of his class, Rayco interned at the World Bank focusing on promoting cooperation between developing countries. His unit was implementing an online platform to share knowledge between teams working in different countries, and Rayco's communications skills were a perfect fit.

With the year flying by and no clear plan for his next steps, Rayco knew that he needed to start connecting with others—to learn about opportunities and perhaps get some help opening doors. That's when I met him through a coaching program for young professionals at the World Bank. Together, Rayco and I designed a networking strategy, approaching his networking as a long-term investment through which he could enrich his professional career, learn and receive help from others, and, at the same time, assist others in their own journey. Rayco began building relationships of different kinds—with promoters who could potentially offer him a job or help him land one, mentors who could provide guidance, role models from whom he could learn, and connectors who could introduce him to other people. Combined, those relationships created a networking tree that even today keeps growing.

While working on this book, I asked him what he thought the key to successful networking is. "It's fundamental to show yourself as you are, to be genuine, to be truly interested in learning from the other person—that's half the job!" Rayco told me.

During this time of intense networking, Rayco developed two relationships that would—through direct and indirect pathways—shape his career. The first was with Jose Luis Ferreyra, a Mexican who led the team in charge of the World Bank's online communications in Spanish. Rayco started to attend events where Jose Luis was a presenter until he managed to speak with him. Rayco also connected with people on Jose Luis's team to understand better what the group did and identify how he could be of help.

Jose Luis was always in search of new ideas and welcomed Rayco's proactive spirit. After several conversations over coffee, Rayco pitched a project that sparked Jose Luis's interest: a series of podcasts featuring end beneficiaries of the World Bank's work in

Latin America. The goal was to portray real people and show the impact of the World Bank in plain language. Rayco's experience would make him the natural lead for the project.

Jose Luis tried for months to get funding but never succeeded. Despite this setback, Jose Luis and Rayco continued to meet regularly, sometimes including others from Jose Luis's team to brainstorm new ideas for collaboration. In that sense, Jose Luis went from being a potential promoter to becoming a role model to Rayco, a person with whom to exchange ideas and from whom he could learn.

The second contact was Richard Miron, a British national, who had worked for the BBC and United Nations before the World Bank, and liked to try innovative ways of communicating using new technologies and storytelling techniques. Richard did not have a team to hire Rayco, but the two enjoyed each other's company, and regularly traded ideas on new ways of communicating. Richard also helped Rayco with his networking by connecting him to other colleagues.

Rayco eventually secured a full-time position at the United Nations Staff System College (UNSSC), an agency that trains UN staff. Based at the campus in Bonn, Germany, Rayco continued to hone his communication and knowledge sharing skills. In fact, he was able to implement some of the ideas he had developed with Jose Luis and Richard. The campus also housed the UNSSC Knowledge Centre for Sustainable Development; there, Rayco learned about climate issues. This was especially poignant for him, as climate is a top concern for the future of the Canary Islands. Rayco remembers his time in Germany as a period of learning, growth, and new relationships. But home was calling.

It took nearly half a year and a lot of networking to find a way to return to his country—meeting people in Germany and other European countries who could offer him remote work, and visiting the Canary Islands to explore local opportunities. Finally, through contacts he had made working on climate issues, he secured several contracts with the UN Environment Programme and returned to his home island to carry out his work remotely. Unfortunately, he soon realized that he felt disconnected from the reality of life in the Canary Islands. He wanted to continue consulting for international organizations and nurture the international network of contacts he had built. But he also wanted to do something that would be meaningful and useful to his birth place.

He found that something through Victor Hernández, a close friend from college, with whom he had stayed in touch over the years. Victor was active in the local branch of the Spanish Socialist Party (Partido Socialista), which promoted progressive policy ideas in the Canary Islands. He suggested Rayco join the party as a volunteer, knowing how useful Rayco's experience in international relations and his relationship-building skills would be.

Rayco began attending meetings. While he recognized that many volunteers tried to use party participation as a fast-track to a paying job, he was more focused on advancing the mission and connecting with like-minded people. When campaign season approached, Victor recommended Rayco to be part of the team supporting the party's senatorial candidate, advising him on communication and climate issues.

These were demanding times for Rayco. He was working long hours as a volunteer while completing two international consultant contracts. But his efforts paid off. The candidate won, and Rayco was asked to become a senior advisor to an elected member of the Canary Island government in charge of climate and land policy. Later, he became the member's cabinet coordinator, leading the entire team of advisors.

Rayco is especially grateful that it was his friend Victor who opened doors for him and recommended him to work on the campaign. "My friend's recommendation was especially touching to me," Rayco says. "We have been friends for years, but he might have wanted the job for himself. However, he thought of me. I am very grateful and hope I can do the same for him and other people in the future."

Rayco's natural curiosity has helped him establish relationships that have enriched him as a person and a professional, and sometimes opened critical doors to jobs and other opportunities. He approaches each relationship as an opportunity to learn and grow, not as a means to get a job. His curiosity has helped him expand his circle of connections, or outer conversation, and with that, his professional horizon. But this is only the beginning for Rayco. "I believe I have a lot to learn from others and want to continue to grow," he says. "But I want to grow with a purpose—make a positive change in the Canary Islands. If I am going to deliver that, it will be thanks to real connections with other people, with them and through them."

KEY TAKEAWAYS

○ Approaching your outer circle with curiosity allows you to learn from others and enrich both your personal and professional lives. First as a student and later as a young professional, Rayco's curiosity helped him establish meaningful relationships, identify opportunities to advance his career, and find purpose.

○ Being genuine helps you connect with people at a deep level and develop long-term professional relationships. In Rayco's words: "It's fundamental to show yourself as you are, to be genuine, to be truly interested in learning from the other person—that's half the job!"

A DIFFERENT TAKE ON NETWORKING
THE CASE OF SAM

S am Hendel is not even 40, but has built an impressive career in the finance industry. Having majored in economics at Yale, Sam has a reputation for sharp insights on the effects of real-time events, such as mergers or pandemics, on financial markets. For instance, when the novel coronavirus was still confined to China, Sam was one of the first analysts to predict that the virus would have a strong impact on the US economy. Recently, he was promoted to president of Levin Easterly, a hedge fund with more than $4 billion under management. He is also the chairman of OkayMedia, which includes OkayPlayer, a music and lifestyle website founded in 1999 by Ahmir (Questlove) Thompson, and OkayAfrica, the leading digital media company focused on African culture.

There's no doubt that Sam's technical skills are top notch. But there is something else that sets him apart: his genuine curiosity about people.

In the business world, and especially in finance, people often approach networking in a transactional way. Professionals try to connect with others in their field who can be "useful" to them— helping them find a new job, close a business deal, or complete whatever immediate objective they are pursuing. Sam prefers a different approach.

"I network without any pretense," Sam readily admits. "I like getting to know people and understanding who they are and what they do. Sometimes that can lead to a business opportunity, a friendship, or nothing ... you never know."

Sam's passion for finance and investing can be traced to his relationship with his father Stephen, a finance professional and Broadway producer. From his father, Sam learned that finance is really about the people behind a business. He enjoys learning about a business model and probing its potential for success. But he especially likes spending time with the people who run a company and getting to know their unique motivation and approach to business.

His skill at building and maintaining relationships has been especially useful in his work as an entrepreneur. Sam is the co-founder of Dataminr, a real-time information analytics company that uses big data to provide early warnings about high-risk events for finance and other sectors.

Sam remembers when his college roommate, Ted Bailey, asked him to help create a data mining company: "Ted has an amazing mind; he thinks differently. He called me and told me that this thing, Twitter, was a gold mine of data, and that we should write code to make sense of it and monetize the information."

Ted had been working for years doing marketing for various large organizations. He had been exploring how new data sources—including social media—could inform marketing strategies. But the big organizations he was working for didn't give him much room to try new business approaches. He was ready for his next career move.

Ted had the vision and business idea. Sam knew the investment landscape and client base. They also needed a data expert. They found one in Jeff Kinsey—another Yale classmate—who had been experimenting with eye-tracking technologies as a software engineer at the Massachusetts Institute of Technology.

The three co-founders, working from a coffee shop near the Lincoln Center in New York City, put together a business plan and started their work to bring in investors. It wouldn't be easy. Sam and his co-founders needed to convince investors to put their money in a company with no track record and an unproven business model based on a combination of artificial intelligence and social media data. And this was all happening in 2009, when the financial crisis had left many businesses bankrupt and had driven the economy into a deep recession. It would be especially difficult to convince investors that any new business would succeed.

But they knew that many investors could also be future consumers of Dataminr, using its real-time insights to help them make other investment decisions. People in finance understood that the world was changing rapidly, and needed razor-sharp tools and data to help them make sound investments. Data and technology experts could provide solutions, but needed the insights from finance professionals on what kind of data they actually needed. Sam, with a foot in both worlds, was a natural bridge.

Sam approached the task as he would any networking activity: seeking meaningful, mutually beneficial connections. Sam understood the importance of listening to investors and creating an environment for them to feel comfortable sharing feedback. "Many investors became our beta testers and gave input to the product improvement as we tailored it to our client needs," Sam told me. With this approach, Dataminr would receive funding while conducting a real-life focus group to better understand what the market needed.

Prospective investors were intrigued by the product—and the chance to make it work for them—and even introduced the trio to other potential investors. Ten years later, Dataminr has more than 650 employees across seven global offices and provides real-time information to thousands of private- and public-sector clients in over 70 countries. It has been recognized by CNBC as one of the world's "most disruptive technology companies" and has a $1.6 billion valuation.

In addition to his work in finance, Sam is helping other young entrepreneurs realize their goals. In 2018, he co-founded Accelerate Yale, an alumni group supporting students with innovative ideas to gain skills, contacts, and funding for their initiatives. "The idea is to provide funding for projects, especially those with potential for high social impact. But it should not be just about money. We should aim at developing lasting connections. Those connections have the potential of real impact."

Sam's genuine interest in people has helped him develop a successful career that spans multiple fields, including finance, technology, media and support of young entrepreneurs. As a finance professional, he understands the importance of strong balance sheets and solid business models. But he also knows that ultimately making a difference depends on connecting with others, building long-lasting relationships, and working together.

KEY TAKEAWAYS

○ Investing time in getting to know others helps you grow as a person and build a meaningful career. Sam approaches networking "without pretense," taking the time to truly connect with people. He engages with others with curiosity and an open mind, which has helped him develop a successful career in finance as well as expand his professional horizon toward other industries.

○ Understanding others' perspectives is critical to help you foster true collaboration. Sam and his Dataminr partners not only asked for investors' money but also spent time listening to them to understand their business needs. That allowed Sam and his partners to improve their product and many investors to benefit from Dataminr as consumers.

LOOKING BACK, LOOKING FORWARD

A genuine leader is not a searcher for consensus, but a molder of consensus.
—*Martin Luther King Jr.*

When we encounter another individual truly as a person, not as an object for use, we become fully human.
—*Martin Buber*

In this book, we have explored how genuine leaders are especially well-positioned to connect with others and facilitate collaboration to transform teams, organizations, and communities. The Expanding Circle framework helps us think about this approach to leadership as a dialectic between our inner and outer circles. Being in harmony with your inner circle and open about who you are is a liberating force. Instead of pretending to be somebody you are not, you feel at ease with yourself and focus on what truly matters to you. Using your inner convictions as a roadmap, you can craft a personal narrative that reflects you and what you care about. Others respect this kind of honesty, and will be quicker to trust and work with you. Chances are that they will also feel inclined to show their real selves, giving you the opportunity to listen to them and get to know them better. That mutual understanding leads directly to a shared purpose and effective collaboration. And as you continue to establish and maintain meaningful relationships, you learn more and more. Over time, your inner circle coalesces with your new experiences and evolves, catalyzing even more significant growth in your outer circle, and propelling you forward on an honest and successful personal, professional, and leadership journey.

For all this to happen, it is essential that you see others and engage with them as human beings (with their own values and ambitions, as well as fears and flaws) and not as mere means to reach your own narrow objectives. In the early 20th century, the philosopher Martin Buber proposed two distinct ways we relate to others: I-It (subject-object) and I-Thou (subject-subject). The I-It encounter describes when we relate to another as object. It might make sense for one-time, transactional interactions, but does not allow for the kind of relationships that will help you find fulfillment while growing and evolving as a human being and leader.

On the other hand, in I-Thou encounters, we relate to each other as authentic beings, without judgment, qualification, or objectification. You care about the other person and try to understand who she or he truly is. You don't try to "use" the other person as a means to an end; rather, you connect and build something together. I-Thou relationships are nurturing. Buber argues that humans deserve to be recognized and treated as such, and that when we recognize others in this way, they become fully human to us and we become fully human to ourselves.

These relationships can also foster true collaboration. They create a bond of trust that helps you find common ground and develop a sense of shared purpose. As we saw in the book's cases, this is essential for people to feel empowered, contribute their best, and help you to expand your influence.

In 2008, Barack Obama became the first African American president of the United States of America. The full story of how he got there is best left to others to tell, but one thing is clear: the unprecedented way Obama engaged with the American public was a key factor in him becoming president. In every conversation, stump speech, town hall, and debate, he led with a genuine, personal narrative, thoughtfully reflecting back the values of his audience. He presented his story as part of the American story.

The son of a black man from Kenya and a white woman from Kansas, Obama connected his own multicultural background to that of the US. He talked about the need to understand each other and work together "to continue the long march of those who came before us, a march for a more just, more equal, more free, more caring and more prosperous America."[16]

During his presidential campaign, Obama recruited an impressive base of young, diverse volunteers, asking them to play an active role, not only in phone banks and canvassing, but also in high-level strategy planning sessions. He wanted volunteers to feel empowered as they campaigned for him. Obama saw his role and that of his professional campaign staff as providing the resources volunteers needed to take initiative and succeed. Especially telling is when, on the night of the Iowa primary, a victorious Obama chose to spend time alone with his young Iowa volunteer leaders. He emerged from the room with tear-laden eyes, showing the depth of involvement and connection between the campaign and its volunteers.

His reliance on these volunteers allowed him to connect with a part of the public that rarely participated in electoral politics, including many African Americans and Latinos—and win them over. He also won over a larger portion of the white vote than any Democratic presidential candidate since 1976.

Obama's case shows us the power of aligning the inner and outer circles. It shows how important it is to connect your personal narrative to a collective one, and to have a strategy that combines communication with relationship building to shape a common course of action. Twelve years later, with two presidential terms under his belt, he talked to a group of students about the power of stories:

"One of the things that I've learned about being a leader is sometimes we think people are motivated only by money, or they're only motivated by power, or these very concrete incentives. But people are also inspired by stories. The stories they tell themselves about what's important and about their lives and about their country and about their communities. And I think if you want to—in whatever field you're in, whether it's business or politics or nonprofit work, it's worthwhile to listen to other people and ask them questions about the stories that are important to them, because oftentimes you'll find their motivations. And when we come together to do important things, it's usually because we told a good story about why we should be working together."[17]

Looking across our own case studies, we can see many of the same themes. Whether they are seasoned leaders with decades of experience or young professionals just beginning their journey, these people have a deep understanding of themselves—including their values, ambitions, and goals. They show their authentic selves. They care about others, engage with others honestly, and lead with generosity—empowering others to fulfill their own ambitions. And many have mastered how to connect their own personal stories to collective narratives that help people work together toward common goals.

For example, Diego's willingness to increase his self-awareness helped him learn from his mistakes and become a better leader, empowering and energizing his teams at Microsoft. When handed a unique opportunity to support young leaders, Fabian approached the experience with an open spirit, ultimately becoming a master connector and champion for youth across the world. Rachel used her personal narrative of activism to transform one of the most traditional international affairs schools. And Alzbeta shaped a collective narrative that changed the way one of the most prestigious international finance institutions managed its investments.

The ability to shape a collective narrative and bring people together toward a common goal is perhaps the most important element these cases have in common. Collective narratives are powerful; they are the backbone of movements. Just think about Sérgio—and how when he invited the East Timorese leadership to be part of the government and work together with the UN officials, he helped foster the full independence of the country. He did not send a dry memo outlining a division of power between the East Timorese leaders and the UN staff. He went to the gathering of the East Timorese revolutionary leaders and framed his invitation as an opportunity to work together to bring dignity and prosperity to people. In fact, he made it clear that they were the real protagonist of the independence process; his role was to support them.

But these grand collective narratives cannot be devised and shaped without first engaging in small actions: listening, asking questions, being curious. Sam's natural inquisitiveness and ability to connect with others allowed him to convince a network of investors and clients to support a startup in the middle of a financial crisis. David immersed himself in Kenyan culture in order to establish strong partnerships with locals and grow his business. And curiosity helped Rayco, a young professional from a family of modest means, build an international professional network and a burgeoning career.

Finally, in all these cases, it was clear that building true, lasting connections with others requires trust. Trust that must be built and continuously nurtured. Avi and Frank are a perfect example—after establishing a trusting bond between themselves, they spent significant time listening to their staff and showing them, with concrete actions, that they cared about them.

The Expanding Circle framework is a tool to help us think about authentic leaders and help you develop your own genuine approach to leadership. What it is not is a universal formula. There is no one way to be a genuine leader. It is up to you to go deep—to explore your inner conversation, find what makes you unique, and decide what is meaningful. The same goes for the outer circle. Pay attention to those around you—seek out opportunities to hear their stories, understand their motivations, and learn from their experiences.

We need genuine leaders now more than ever. We live in a world that is full of uncertainty. Organizations need to constantly adapt to keep up with market dynamics—sometimes at the expense of their employees. Businesses focus on efficiency, but often fail to create an environment in which people feel they belong. And in the digital economy and globalized markets, organizations tend to be decentralized, making it difficult for workers to create meaningful relationships with others.

In this world, people crave leaders who see them as human beings, not just as economic resources. They want leaders who listen to them and create space for them to develop as professionals. People want to be part of something bigger than themselves. Leaders need to be able to provide that sense of purpose. They should be good communicators and articulate a collective narrative that resonates with others. They should set the strategic direction, and then empower their staff to get the job done. Leaders should be great listeners and ask the right questions. And to do all that, they need to tune in—to themselves, to others, to the world around them.

After 15 years in the United States, my wife, Michelle, and I decided to take some time off and moved temporarily to Argentina, my home country. She would build up her Spanish and gain some professional experience working abroad. I would take time to write this book and plan my next career move. Our two-year-old son, Eli, would continue to do what all two-year-olds do—delight and irritate his parents in equal measure.

For the first few months, all went as planned, until the COVID-19 crisis happened.

As I was finishing the interviews and preparing the first draft of the manuscript, the virus was beginning to spread around the world. It disrupted all aspects of life, and incited widescale fear and uncertainty. It has already taken hundreds of thousands of lives. It has also forced us all to think hard about what kind of world we want to live in—and what kind of leaders we want to follow.

In the early days of the pandemic, citizens largely supported their national leaders and looked to them for wisdom and guidance. However, when it became difficult to see how and when the nightmare would end—when people continued to die and the economic damage became more evident—many began to question the capacity of their leaders to navigate the crisis. People lost trust in those who seemed to play politics and manipulate public opinion. But they continued to support those leaders who had created a genuine connection with them, dared to tell them the hard truths, and demonstrated they were doing their best to implement thorough policies.

COVID-19 challenged leaders in all sectors of society—and demonstrated that we need good leadership across the board. Think about a hospital director trying to support and protect her staff who were risking their own lives with insufficient resources. Or a small business owner who had to close his doors overnight and struggle to keep his employees on the payroll. Or perhaps even the president of a videoconferencing company that saw his business balloon overnight, but also had to face unexpected public scrutiny and an increased volume of customer demands.

During the crisis, Michelle, Eli, and I were locked down at home. Our two-bedroom apartment became a sort of preschool, as we tried to help Eli continue his life as normally as possible. We worked during his naps or late at night. It was exhausting, but honestly a small inconvenience compared to the experiences of those who were facing the devastating health and economic effects of the virus.

After more than three months, the government eased some of the restrictions and began to allow people to go outside for exercise. I took Eli to a nearby park with a duck pond—Eli loves feeding them. As he started to throw small pieces of bread and the ducks paddled closer, I noticed the ripple effect of the bread on the water—expanding waves, expanding circles. Eli was elated—his small arm going back and forth, back and forth—throwing the bread again and again. The circles kept expanding through the water. The moment was one of simple joy, bursting with life.

After so many months working on this book and seeing the importance of leadership during the COVID-19 crisis, I can't help thinking about the leadership of the future. I wonder what kind of leaders will emerge from future generations, how they will communicate and connect with people. I think about the responsibility that we have to our own children to grow up in a healthy and stimulating environment. I think about the role we can play in fostering their curiosity about themselves and others. I hope that our children grow up in a world where people take these lessons to heart, and communicate and connect with each other in a genuine way. That, I believe, is the root of true leadership—the only kind we will ever need.

APPENDIX

Everything should be made as simple as possible, but not simpler.
—Albert Einstein

COMPLEX IDEAS: SIMPLE PRESENTATIONS

The original version of this article was written jointly with Paul McClure, senior editor at the World Bank. This version includes minor updates to make it more relevant to the readers of this book.

A s communications specialists at an international development institution, we work with a range of technical experts—economists, financial analysts, social scientists, and so on. These experts spend a lot of time developing ideas, but they often don't invest enough time in presenting their ideas effectively. A lot of great thinking gets lost in translation because experts don't make it accessible to audiences who aren't experts in their field. And these can be the most important audiences—decisionmakers, investors, and public opinion influencers.

Too often, we've seen thoughtful analyses and cutting-edge ideas getting bogged down in text-heavy slides. We've seen audiences sitting through long presentations who are clearly more interested in their smartphones than in what the experts have to say. But we have also seen how some experts invest extra time in preparing their presentations, effectively sharing their work and influencing the people that matter. Here are some key factors for presenting complex, technical ideas effectively.

SET CLEAR OBJECTIVES

Define what you want to accomplish and align the whole presentation to support your goals. Often, people set vague objectives such as "increase awareness." You need to be much more concrete.

Think about behaviors: What would you like your audience to do or think, as a result of your presentation?

SEE YOUR WORK AS YOUR AUDIENCE DOES

Things that make sense to you may not be clear to your audience without some guidance. Try to understand where they are coming from, and tailor your points to them. Define your audience, going beyond broad labels such as "senior management," "engineers," or "accountants." Be more specific. Try to understand what's on their minds, what keeps them up at night, what success means for them. And most importantly, what they can hope to get from your presentation.

FIT CONTENT TO THE FORMAT

How much time will you have? The shorter the presentation, the easier it will be to keep your audience's attention. But don't rush to fit a large number of details in a few minutes. Keep your presentation focused on one subject and a few main points.

IDENTIFY YOUR MAIN IDEA

You can present your work in many ways, highlighting various aspects of it. But you need to be clear about the main idea you want to convey as a "take-away" for the audience. A good overarching message might be something new, perhaps surprising or counter-intuitive, a challenge to a belief, an old idea in a new light. You don't have to be the expert on your topic, but you have to be an expert.

MAKE SURE YOUR MAIN IDEA IS CLEAR AND SIMPLE

Write it down in one or two sentences. Ask yourself: Is my main point new? Is it interesting to my audience? Can it be implemented or be useful to them? If you can't articulate your main idea succinctly, or if you find yourself answering "no" to any of these questions, keep refining it.

MAKE AN OUTLINE AND DEFINE A FEW KEY MESSAGES

There isn't one best structure that works for all presentations, but there are some general principles that usually work.

○ *Make your audience care.* Show your passion. Audiences will forgive you if you look nervous or forget a fact. But they won't care about what you have to say unless you care. Use stories and analogies your audience can relate to.

○ *Explain your idea, clearly and with conviction.* Focus on the "so what." Make sure the audience understands the implications of your work, and its importance—especially how it affects them.

○ *Focus on clear and compelling evidence.* Make sure your audience can understand your supporting evidence. The aim is for them to absorb your ideas, not to show how much work you have done. Trim down to the essentials; too many details can distract from your key points.

○ *Tell stories, backed by data.* People are wired to learn through stories. Where possible, use data to tell a story that resonates both intellectually and emotionally with your audience. Stories can be a bridge between data and those who need to learn from it, or make decisions based on it. Data with a good story is unforgettable.

○ *Include a call to action.* What do you want your audience to do after your presentation? Approve a project? Decide on a policy? Invest in something? To motivate your audience, make clear why they need to do what you're asking them to do. Whatever approach you choose, remember that your goal is to communicate your work effectively. You can use stories and emotions, but those are tools for conveying your points, not goals in themselves.

CREATE SLIDES ONLY AS NEEDED (AND KEEP THEM SIMPLE!)

Your presentation is you speaking to your audience, not the PowerPoint, Prezi, or other file on the screen. Use slides if necessary to clarify information, but don't let them become the sole focus or a distraction to the audience. Slides won't do the talking for you, and they can't replace in-depth materials you might want the audience to read. If you include a lot of text, your audience will want to read your slides, looking over your shoulder instead of listening to you.

USE BRIEF, STRAIGHTFORWARD TEXT

To highlight key points, use accessible language and short phrases. Follow the "rule of six": up to six lines per slide, up to six words per line. Focus on just one main message per slide. A good image or graph is usually more memorable than a bullet point. Keep slides simple and clear, even if the concept is complex. Think about billboards on a highway, which let drivers grasp key messages at a glance. You want your audience to absorb information from a slide quickly and then pay attention to what you're saying.

DON'T CREATE A REPORT

Presentations are a direct effort to engage with an audience face to face, serving as the bridge to a more comprehensive analysis found in a report. Presentations can certainly appeal to the intellect, but they can also elicit an emotional response through the use of storytelling, compelling visuals, and perhaps your sense of humor. Ideally you can supplement the presentation with material for people to read on their own. But you can also use the speaking notes for the details, and if somebody needs to "read the presentation" you can send it as a PDF, making the notes visible.

REHEARSE

It takes practice to be on message and look natural during a presentation. While a small number of people are natural performers, for most of us, practice is fundamental to feeling at ease in front of a group and having the right words at our command. Rehearse in front of others—colleagues, friends. Ask for their feedback, learn from it, and keep practicing.

BE PRESENT

Focus on connecting with the audience, not on the formal aspects of "giving a presentation." After all, successful presentations are conversations in which you tell other people your ideas, share your work, and prompt them to take action. Maintain a natural tone of voice—if needed, use a microphone. Make eye contact. Remember that you're usually not the only expert in the room, and that you may be able to learn from others as well.

STAY FLEXIBLE

While you can state upfront that you prefer to present first and then take questions, don't be afraid to adapt and respond to comments or questions. For the audience, this may be the most valuable part of the session, so be careful not to undermine it by suggesting that a question made the presentation run over or forced you to rush. It's usually more important that the information you cover is absorbed than that you cover everything you've prepared. If you run long, feel free to set aside some of your slides. You can follow up with the audience afterward, with the presentation or other materials they can read on their own.

And one more thing: Your last slide matters

Your final slide will be on screen for a long time, often for the entire discussion that follows the presentation. Think of this slide as an opportunity to display content that reinforces your main message. Avoid including filler text like "Questions?" or "Thank You."

ENDNOTES

1. Samantha Power. *Chasing the Flame: One Man's Fight to Save the World.* (New York: Penguin, 2008). Other quotes from Xanana Gusmão for this story belong to Power's book too. The story is also informed by interviews conducted for this book with Fabrizio Hochschild-Drummond, special adviser to the UN Secretary-General, who served as Sérgio Viera de Mello's chief of staff in East Timor; and with Carolina Larreira, Sérgio's spouse and UN team member in both East Timor and Iraq.

2. Yuval Harari. "What Explains the Rise of Humans?" Presentation, TED Global London, June 2015. https://www.ted.com/talks/yuval_noah_harari_what_explains_the_rise_of_humans/transcript?language=en

3. Douglas Ready. "The Power of a Clear Leadership Narrative." *MIT Sloan Management Review*, September 23, 2019. https://sloanreview.mit.edu/article/the-power-of-a-clear-leadership-narrative/

4. This approach to leadership is in line with the work of Harvard Professor William George who highlights the importance of leaders driven by values.

5. Gallup. "State of the American Workplace." 2017. https://www.gallup.com/workplace/238085/state-american-work-place-report-2017.aspx

6. In fact, the most surprising results were from the primary elections. In Argentina, all parties conduct their primaries simultaneously. The primaries are open and mandatory, meaning that all eligible citizens are required to vote. In practice, political parties present only one candidate (at least for the top positions) and therefore the primaries became the first round of the general elections.

7. Simon Sinek, in his book *Start with Why*, uses these categories to think about leadership in general. I find them especially helpful to develop a professional narrative.

8. News Staff. "Rachel Kyte Named Fletcher School Dean." *Tufts Now*, April 8, 2019. https://now.tufts.edu/articles/rachel-kyte-named-fletcher-school-dean

9. Valerie Wencis. "A Conversation with Rachel Kyte, New Dean of the Fletcher School." *Tufts Now*, June 21, 2019. https://now.tufts.edu/articles/meet-new-fletcher-school-dean

10. Shawn Ghuman. "The Future of Fletcher: An Interview with Dean Rachel Kyte." *The Fletcher Forum of World Affairs*, December 1, 2019. http://www.fletcherforum.org/home/2019/12/1/the-future-of-fletcher-an-interview-with-dean-rachel-kyte

11. Wencis. "A Conversation"

12. Tal Eyal, Mary Steffel, and Nicholas Epley. "Perspective-Taking Doesn't Help You Understand What Others Want." Harvard Business Review, October 9, 2018. https://hbr.

org/2018/10/research-perspective-taking-doesnt-help-you-understand-what-others-want

13. Emily Pronin, Justin Kruger, Kenneth Savitsky, and Lee Ross. "You Don't Know Me, But I Know You: The Illusion of Asymmetric Insight." *Journal of Personality and Social Psychology* 81, no. 4 (2001): 639-656. https://pubmed.ncbi.nlm.nih.gov/11642351/

14. Dale Carnegie. How to Win Friends and Influence People, 80th anniversary ed. (New York: Simon & Schuster, 2009), 26.

15. Eventually, their business grew so much that they had to move their manufacturing operations to an industrial park, but kept a strong presence in the slum.

16. Barack Obama. "A More Perfect Union." Remarks, Constitution Center, Philadelphia, PA, March 18, 2008. https://www.npr.org/templates/story/story.php?storyId=88478467

17. Barack Obama. Remarks, YSEALI Town Hall, Ho Chi Minh City, Vietnam, May 25, 2016. https://obamawhitehouse.archives.gov/the-press-office/2016/05/25/remarks-president-obama-yseali-town-hall

REFERENCES

Bekerman, Diego. "El Día Que El Caballo Perdió Su Trabajo." Presentation, filmed May 14, 2019 at Retail Day Expo, Buenos Aires. https://www.youtube.com/watch?v=FBKeFahaHAA

Bekerman, Diego. Presentation, filmed September 7, 2016 at Fuckup Nights, Buenos Aires V. VII, Buenos Aires. https://www.youtube.com/watch?v=pm8TJj8ZCbg

Buber, Martin. *I and Thou*. Edinburgh: T. & T. Clark, 1937.

Carnegie, Dale. *How to Win Friends and Influence People,* 80th anniversary ed. New York: Simon & Schuster, 2009.

Eyal, Tal, Mary Steffel, and Nicholas Epley. "Perspective-Taking Doesn't Help You Understand What Others Want." *Harvard Business Review*, October 9, 2018. https://hbr.org/2018/10/research-perspective-taking-doesnt-help-you-understand-what-others-want

Ferrazzi, Keith and Tahl Raz. *Never Eat Alone and Other Secrets to Success: One Relationship at a Time*. New York: Currency Doubleday, 2005.

Frankl, Viktor. *Man's Search for Meaning: An Introduction to Logotherapy.* New York: Simon & Schuster, 1984.

Gallup. "State of the American Workplace." 2017. https://www.gallup.com/workplace/238085/state-american-workplace-report-2017.aspx

Gan, Muping, Daniel Heller, and Serena Chen. "The Power in Being Yourself: Feeling Authentic Enhances the Sense of Power." *Personality and Social Psychology Bulletin* 44, no. 10 (2018): 1460-1472. https://doi.org/10.1177/0146167218771000

Ganz, Marshall. "Public Narrative, Collective Action, and Power." In *Accountability Through Public Opinion: From Inertia to Public Action,* edited by Sina Odugbemi and Taeku Lee: 273-289. Washington, D.C: The World Bank, 2011.

George, William. *Authentic Leadership: Rediscovering the Secrets to Creating Lasting Value.* San Francisco: Jossey-Bass, 2003.

Ghuman, Shawn. "The Future of Fletcher: An Interview with Dean Rachel Kyte." *The Fletcher Forum of World Affairs,* December 1, 2019. http://www.fletcherforum.org/home/2019/12/1/the-future-of-fletcher-an-interview-with-dean-rachel-kyte

Gino, Francesca, Ovul Sezer, and Laura Huang. "To Be or Not to Be Your Authentic Self? Catering to Others' Preferences Hinders Performance." *Organizational Behavior and Human Decision Processes* 158. (2020): 83-100. https://doi.org/10.1016/j.obhdp.2020.01.003

Harari, Yuval. *Sapiens: A Brief History of Humankind.* New York: Harper, 2015.

Harari, Yuval. "What Explains the Rise of Humans?" Presentation, TED Global London, June 2015. https://www.ted.com/talks/yuval_noah_harari_what_explains_the_rise_of_humans/transcript?language=en

Hochschild, Fabrizio. "In and Above Conflict: A Study on Leadership in the United Nations." *Centre for Humanitarian Dialogue.* July, 2010. https://www.hdcentre.org/publications/in-and-above-conflict-a-study-on-leadership-in-the-united-nations/

Kimsey-House, Henry, Karen Kimsey-House, and Philip Sandahl. *Co-Active Coaching: Changing Business, Transforming Lives.* Boston: Nicholas Brealey Publishing, 2011.

Koss, Fabian A. "Children Falling into the Digital Divide." *Journal of International Affairs 55*, no 1. (2001): 75-90. https://www.jstor.org/stable/24357671

Koss, Fabian A. "GOOOOOL ... (for development). Donors and businesses are realizing the social and economic development benefits of sports." *Americas Quarterly AQ / Americas Society Council of the Americas* (2011).

Kotter, John. *On What Leaders Really Do.* Boston: Harvard Business School Press, 1999.

Kuhn, David. "Exit Polls: How Obama Won." *Politico,* November 5, 2008. https://www.politico.com/story/2008/11/exit-polls-how-obama-won-015297

News Staff. "Rachel Kyte Named Fletcher School Dean." *Tufts Now,* April 8, 2019. https://now.tufts.edu/articles/rachel-kyte-named-fletcher-school-dean

Obama, Barack. Keynote Address, Democratic National Convention, July 27, 2004. https://www.pbs.org/newshour/show/barack-obamas-keynote-address-at-the-2004-democratic-national-convention

Obama, Barack. "A More Perfect Union." Remarks, Constitution Center, Philadelphia, PA, March 18, 2008. https://www.npr.org/templates/story/story.php?storyId=88478467

Obama, Barack. Remarks, YSEALI Town Hall, Ho Chi Minh City, Vietnam, May 25, 2016. https://obamawhitehouse.archives.gov/the-press-office/2016/05/25/remarks-president-obama-yseali-town-hall

Plouffe, David. The Audacity to Win: The Inside Story and Lessons of Barack Obama's Historic Victory. New York: Penguin, 2009.

Power, Samantha. Chasing the Flame: One Man's Fight to Save the World. New York: Penguin, 2008.

Pronin, Emily, Justin Kruger, Kenneth Savitsky, and Lee Ross. "You Don't Know Me, But I Know You: The Illusion of Asymmetric Insight." Journal of Personality and Social Psychology 81, no. 4 (2001): 639-656. https://pubmed.ncbi.nlm.nih.gov/11642351/

Ready, Douglas. "The Power of a Clear Leadership Narrative." MIT Sloan Management Review, September 23, 2019. https://sloanreview.mit.edu/article/the-power-of-a-clear-leadership-narrative/

Ready, Douglas, Carol Cohen, David Kiron, and Benjamin Pring. "The New Leadership Playbook for the Digital Age." MIT Sloan Management Review, January 2020. https://sloanreview.mit.edu/projects/the-new-leadership-playbook-for-the-digital-age/

Sinek, Simon. *Start With Why: How Great Leaders Inspire Everyone to Take Action.* New York: Penguin, 2009.

Wencis, Valerie. "A Conversation with Rachel Kyte, New Dean of the Fletcher School." *Tufts Now,* June 21, 2019. https://now.tufts.edu/articles/meet-new-fletcher-school-dean

INTERVIEWS

I am deeply grateful to the more than three dozen leaders, high-performing professionals, and subject matter experts that spent time talking to me as I researched this book. All of these conversations have been very valuable, and some of them informed stories featured in the book. My special thanks to:

David Auerbach, Co-founder, Sanergy

Rayco Bejarano, Advisor and Cabinet Coordinator, Government of the Canary Islands

Diego Bekerman, General Manager for Small, Medium and Corporate Customers in Latin America and the Caribbean, Microsoft

Norma Gonzalez, Director, Fulbright Commission in Argentina

Sam Hendel, President, Levin Easterly Partners; Co-founder, Dataminr; Co-founder, Accelerate Yale

Fabrizio Hochschild, Special Adviser to the UN Secretary General and former Chief of Staff for Sérgio Vieira de Mello in East Timor, United Nations

Avi Hoffman, former Risk Management Co-director, International Finance Corporation, The World Bank Group

Alzbeta Klein, Director of Climate Business and former Director of Portfolio Management, International Finance Corporation, The World Bank Group

Fabian Koss, Founder, KC Social Impact Lab; former Senior Executive, Inter-American Development Bank

Rachel Kyte, Dean, The Fletcher School of Law and Diplomacy at Tufts; former Special Representative of the UN Secretary-General for Sustainable Energy, United Nations; former Vice President, The World Bank Group

Carolina Larreira, Founder, Centro Sérgio Viera de Mello; former member of Sérgio Viera de Mello's teams in East Timor and Iraq, United Nations; Sérgio Viera de Mello's spouse

Frank Taverner, former Risk Management Co-director, International Finance Corporation, The World Bank Group

ABOUT THE EDITOR

JILLIAN WEST is a freelance communications strategist, writer, and editor. Her work focuses on health care policy, patient safety, and the social determinants of health and health equity. Previously, she worked at the Urban Institute, a research organization informing public policy and practice; The Leapfrog Group, a nonprofit watchdog group using transparent public reporting to improve safety and quality in US hospitals; and The National Academy of Medicine.

She received her bachelor's degree in psychology from Macalester College and a master's degree in strategic communication from American University.

She currently lives just outside Annapolis, Maryland with her husband and two children.